Praise for Postcards From Babylon

If I had miraculous powers, I would interrupt the programming of every religious broadcast in America, then, as Jesus replaced water with wine, I would substitute the message from Brian Zahnd that you'll read in this book. Read it and you'll see why. I recommend that you buy two copies of this book. Immediately read one—underline it and extract quotes from it to share on Facebook and Twitter, and refer to it in sermons and casual conversations. Send the other to that friend or relative who likes to talk about God and country. Include a note asking if they'd be willing to talk with you about it after they read it. Then see what happens as these *Postcards from Babylon* do their work in you and in others.

—Brian D. McLaren, author of *The Great Spiritual Migration*

This love letter from a concerned pastor will enrage contemporary Pharaohs and their false prophets who blaspheme by blessing everything that Christ came to free us from. *Postcards from Babylon* diagnoses the diabolical and invites us to become pilgrims on Christ's narrow road that delivers us out into life.

—Jarrod McKenna, pastor, founder of First Home Project for refugees in Australia

Now in a bold and daring articulation, Brian Zahnd has sketched a "Theology of the Cross" for our time and place in the United States of the twenty-first century. He does so in a way that deeply resonates with the primal claims of evangelical theology. He sees that the Gospel is inherently and inescapably countercultural because the God of the Gospel is in particular and passionate solidarity with the "left behind."

—Walter Brueggemann, Columbia Theological Seminary

POSTCARDS

FROM BABYLON

The Church In American Exile

Brian Zahnd

For Jude, Mercy, Finn, Hope, Evey, Pax, and Liam.

I want to do all I can to help make Christianity possible for you and your generation. This book is part of that attempt.

"She who is in Babylon greets you."
—1 Peter 5:13

CONTENTS

FOREWORD

As long ago as the sixteenth century, Martin Luther boldly voiced a vigorous either/or for Christian faith in terms of a "Theology of Glory" and a "Theology of the Cross." By the former Luther referred to an articulation of Gospel faith that smacked of triumphalism that was allied with worldly power that specialized in winning, control, being first, and being best. For Luther, that theology was all tied up with the European imperial of his time. By the contrast of a "Theology of the Cross," Luther referred to the risky way of Jesus that is marked by humility, obedience, and vulnerability standing in sharp contrast to and in opposition to the hunger for "Glory." The "way of the cross," for Luther, is demanding and costly because it contradicts the dominant way of the world.

Now in a bold and daring articulation, Brian Zahnd has sketched a "Theology of the Cross" for our time and place in the United States of the twenty-first century. He does so in a way that deeply resonates with the primal claims of evangelical theology. He sees that the Gospel is inherently and inescapably countercultural because the God of the Gospel is in particular and passionate solidarity with the "left behind."

In this daring articulation, Zahnd pulls no punches. He sees that so much of the American church has been cozily allied with the high claims of U.S. nationalism that readily tilts toward imperialism. The whole package of dominant triumphalist faith adds up to "God and country," with "country" being the tail that wags the dog of "God." Most particularly, this triumphalist alliance has a long history of attachment to military ideology, the winning of wars, and the domination of other nations and their resources and markets. In one of his many poetic renderings, Zahnd offers a nearly unbearable riff on the aggression of Achilles in the *Iliad* and completes the thought of Homer as he enumerates at great length the inventory of wars in which triumphalist Christianity has been eagerly and characteristically implicated. That long alliance with brutalizing power of course has deeply skewed everything in the faith, offering both a caricature of the God of the Gospel and a distorted notion of both discipleship and of citizenship. Before he finishes, Zahnd goes on to see how it is that the Trump administration is a near perfect embodiment of that ideology of "lust, greed, and pride" and how so much of the church has sadly colluded with the Trump administration in a pretend embrace of Gospel faith.

His manuscript pivots on the theme of exile because faithful obedience to the Lord of the Cross inevitably makes his followers outsiders to the empire world of "Glory." It was as punishment (so the text avers) that God's chosen ended in Babylon in exile. It turns out, however, that that scene of displacement was an unexpected opportunity for that ancient chosen people of God to recover vocation and to re-embrace a clear vision of what it meant (and means) to be chosen by the Lord of vulnerability. The concrete historical reference to "exile" in the biblical text becomes, for both biblical tradition and for this author, a metaphor for the characteristic location of the displaced from the force of empire.

The more I learn of Zahnd's work, the more I have deep respect and appreciation for his truth-telling. This book is a reprimand and an invitation to his fellow evangelicals about how the way has been lost and what it will mean to "come home," because it is a gift to come down where we ought to be! Beyond his more immediate circle, however, Zahnd addresses all of us, because all of us in the Christian community in the U.S. are too readily narcotized by the mantras of Caesar, Herod, Constantine, and their continuing heirs. The exposé and ending of triumphalism in the church is a huge piece of work. Zahnd leaves no doubt that it is now our proper work that will require sustained energy and courage. It is, however, the only way to get to Easter liberty wherein the empire of death is known to be fake. The empire saturates us with the fake news of "Glory." This book exposes those false promises because the way of empire can never make us safe or happy. This book also invites us to the good news of Gospel truth. The signature mark of Zahnd's work is his poetic idiom that permits us fresh access to that emancipatory truth. This is indeed a postcard sent from our exilic habitat. It is filled with the news for which we have been waiting!

Walter Brueggemann
Columbia Theological Seminary
August 7, 2018

CHAPTER 1

CONVERSION, CATACOMBS, AND A COUNTERCULTURE

I lived with them on Montague Street
In a basement down the stairs
There was music in the cafés at night
And revolution in the air
—*Bob Dylan, "Tangled Up In Blue"*

t was a Saturday morning, and I awoke to "Tangled Up In Blue" on the radio. It was the first time I'd really paid any attention to a Dylan song. I was mesmerized by the wild poetry that told a disjointed story with every verse ending with someone "tangled up in blue"—whatever that meant. I spent the day playing basketball and that evening went with a group of high school friends to a youth rally at the local college sponsored by the Fellowship of Christian Athletes. I'd grown up in church so this wasn't particularly novel. I had no expectations beyond an evening of hanging out with friends…especially a girl I had my eye on. I remember what I wore that night—big bell Levi's, Converse All-Stars, and a pink cowboy shirt. Stylin'. At the youth rally, a band that couldn't really rock was playing squeaky clean Christian music that I thought was pretty lame. I was beginning to regret spending my Saturday night in a churchy way.

Then without warning Jesus came crashing in! I have no other way of explaining it. The speaker invited us to open our lives to Jesus, and when I cracked the door open with a simple prayer, Jesus charged in and suddenly became the most real thing in my life. In the "twinkling of an eye" Jesus went from being a benign religious figure on the periphery of my cultural existence to being the epicenter of all that mattered. It was the kind of bolt-out-of-the-blue phenomenon you hear about but that seems more legendary than credible. I never dreamed that such a thing could happen to me. I was interested in rock and roll, basketball, and girls, not religious conversions. But it happened. I had been struck by lightning.

After the youth rally I went with my friends to McDonald's, but I was in no mood to socialize. I was still trying to process what had happened. I wouldn't have said, "I got saved." That wasn't how I thought about it. I had always believed in Jesus in a generic Christian way. I had been baptized when I was eight. I was familiar with the Bible stories and could even recite the sixty-six books of the Bible in order—a trick we learned in Sunday School. I didn't think I had suddenly become a Christian; it was more like I had just been overwhelmed with the undeniable reality of Jesus Christ. It seemed like the truth of Jesus was placing a demand upon my own life. So I sat by myself, not talking to anyone, trying to take it in. I got home around midnight. As I walked into my basement bedroom, the room was filled with a strange light that didn't seem to come from anywhere—it was more like the room was immersed in light. I fell to my knees, lifted my hands, and worshiped Jesus. I had never done anything like this before. I know it all sounds a bit fantastic, and I won't blame you for being somewhat incredulous, but it happened. And nothing remotely like this had ever happened before.

This was my conversion experience—if that's what it was. To this day I don't have a precise label for what happened that night, which is fine, because categorizing spiritual experiences is mostly a bad habit. It's probably enough to say that was the night I encountered Jesus in a new way. Though the elements of Christianity had always been present in my life, this was the moment when everything detonated and my lifelong fascination with Jesus began. It was my Damascus Road, my Mount of Transfiguration, my Isle of Patmos revelation. I don't think most people need to meet Jesus in such a dramatic fashion, but for whatever reason that's how it happened for me.

When I went back to school on Monday, I took a Bible with me. I grabbed it off my father's bookshelf where there was a collection of Bibles in different translations. At random I picked a red paperback edition of the New English Bible. I didn't do this to make a statement or to be noticed, but for the simple reason that I wanted to read it. Of course carrying a Bible to school *did* get noticed. Overnight I went from being the high school Led Zeppelin freak to the high school Jesus freak. In those days everyone called me Fry—a nickname given to me in grade school by Richard Flanagan in tribute to my fiery temper. A few weeks after my dramatic encounter with Jesus, people began to say, "Man, Fry, I can't believe what's happened to you!" I'd say, "I can't either…but it happened!" Within a few months I was leading morning Bible studies in the high school gym and evening Bible studies in my parent's basement. I had become the *de facto* pastor to a group of teenage disciples. It's no exaggeration to say I've been doing the work of a pastor since I was seventeen. Or as I like to say it, I've been a pastor longer than I've been an adult! That's probably not a good idea and it's certainly not a pattern to follow, but it's what happened.

This was all during the heady days of the Jesus Movement—the Jesus-centered spiritual movement that began among countercultural young people in California, spread across the country and eventually became significant enough to be featured on the cover of *Time* magazine. The center of the Jesus Movement in St. Joseph, Missouri was the Catacombs—a Christian coffeehouse in the basement of a dive bar in a seedy part of town. The Catacombs was mostly a music venue for the emerging Jesus Music scene. We usually hosted local Christian artists, but occasionally nationally known artists like Keith Green, Second Chapter of Acts, and Sweet Comfort Band would play the Catacombs.

The Catacombs was an apt name for our Jesus Movement coffeehouse—it spoke both of our dingy, subterranean venue and the connection we felt to early Christianity. The catacombs in Rome are the underground labyrinths created by the early Christians for the burial of believers and occasionally for Eucharistic worship. The Roman catacombs have become a kind of symbol for pre-Constantine Christianity, a subversive underground movement challenging the idolatrous claims of empire, a dangerous countercultural society confessing that because Jesus is Lord, Caesar is not. Christians praying underground in the Catacombs and Christians martyred above ground in the Coliseum have become the two enduring icons of the Christianity that predates Christendom.

For various reasons, those of us who were part of the Jesus Movement of the 1970s felt a connection with the Jesus Movement of the AD 70s. We may not have been thrown to the lions, but we had a very distinct sense that we belonged to a Christian counterculture. We liked to believe we represented a more radical version of Christianity than you would likely find in your local Baptist or Catholic church. Sure, a lot of this was youthful naiveté with a dose of adolescent arrogance, but forty years later I can honestly say there was a grain of truth to it. We may have been young, naive, and a bit too cocky, but we were also undeniably countercultural. We didn't see Christianity as a form of civic religion in service of American values but as a direct challenge to the assumed cultural values of America.

The Jesus Movement, like its secular predecessor, the hippie movement, was markedly non-materialistic. Granted, it's a lot easier to be non-materialistic when all you own is a pair of blue jeans, a couple of t-shirts, and a record collection. Those were the days before mortgages, maternity bills, and IRAs. But the point is we didn't shy away from the jarring passages in the Gospels where Jesus says uncomfortable things like "None of you can become my disciple if you do not give up all your possessions."[1]

The Jesus Movement also carried a strong antiwar sentiment. We were pro-peace and antiwar, not because John Lennon sang about it in "Imagine," but because Jesus preached about it in the Sermon on the Mount. Perhaps the best thing I can say about the Jesus Movement is that it took the Sermon on the Mount seriously. While many Protestant and Catholic theologians during Christendom had so nuanced the Sermon on the Mount that it had become pedestrian and prosaic, a bunch of long-haired Jesus freaks were realizing that the Sermon on the Mount was thrilling, demanding, and dangerous as dynamite. The Jesus

Movement was making Jesus revolutionary again. Indeed a common Jesus Movement motif was to represent Jesus as a kind of outlaw. A familiar poster had a picture of Jesus with these words:

WANTED:
JESUS CHRIST

ALIAS: THE MESSIAH, THE SON OF GOD, KING OF KINGS, LORD OF LORDS, PRINCE OF PEACE, ETC.

Notorious leader of an underground liberation movement.

Wanted for the following charges:

Practicing medicine, winemaking,
and food distribution without a license.

Interfering with businessmen in the temple.

Associating with known criminals, radicals,
subversives, prostitutes, and street people.

APPEARANCE:
Typical hippie type—long hair, beard, robe, sandals.

Hangs around slum areas, few rich friends,
often sneaks out into the desert.

BEWARE:
This man is extremely dangerous.

His insidiously inflammatory message is particularly dangerous
to young people who haven't been taught to ignore him yet.

WARNING! HE IS STILL AT LARGE!

If you are inclined to dismiss this as just another example of Christian kitsch, I would urge you not to. While there was obviously an element of playfulness in this poster, it actually made a serious point—a point the Jesus Movement had a correct instinct about. The Jesus of the Gospels is far more suited for an F.B.I. Wanted poster than for being the poster child of American values. While the historical Jesus certainly wasn't a hippie, he was obviously dangerous and subversive. After all, Rome didn't crucify people for extolling civic virtues and pledging allegiance to the empire. In announcing and enacting the kingdom of God, Jesus was countercultural and counter-imperial. This is why Jesus was crucified. His crime was claiming to be a king who had not been installed by Caesar.

The counterculture nature of the kingdom of God was a chief characteristic of the Jesus Movement—both the original one and the one that swept America in the 1970s. The early Christians of the catacombs knew that in following Jesus they would often be in opposition to the values that the Roman elite and the Roman legions stood for. And those of us at the 1970s Catacombs knew that what Jesus represented did not have an easy fit with the materialism and militarism of American culture. If anything, what Jesus taught was an out-and-out repudiation of American materialism and militarism. The Jesus Movement was no longer content with the docile and domesticated sermons of Mayberry. We weren't interested in making Jesus safe and palatable for suburban consumers. We knew that Jesus was radical and that his message was revolutionary. We weren't being countercultural to be avant-garde; we were being countercultural because the gospel demanded it! We weren't being countercultural to imitate hippies; we were being countercultural to imitate Jesus!

Forty years later when I read Larry Hurtado's *Destroyer of the Gods: Early Christian Distinctiveness in the Roman World* and Alan Kreider's *The Patient Ferment of the Early Church: The Improbable Rise of Christianity in the Roman Empire*, both attempts at capturing the ethos and praxis of the early church, I was surprised at how often what these scholars had to say about pre-Constantine Christianity called to mind memories from the Jesus Movement. Like the early church that I read about in the books of Hurtado and Kreider, we too had an almost fanatical obsession with Jesus, a clear disdain for materialism, a Sermon on the Mount-inspired opposition to war, a penchant for communal life, and a deep ambivalence toward political parties. In following Jesus we knew we were going against the grain of post-WWII American assumptions. In a word, we were countercultural.

In a culture that venerates materialism and militarism, the only way to truly follow Jesus is to be countercultural. Sure, the prosperity gospel extols materialism and the religious right celebrates militarism, but these are nothing but attempts to smuggle the idols of Mammon and Mars into Christianity. A synchronistic religion that attempts to amalgamate Jesus and American values may be popular, but it's unfaithful to the Spirit who calls the people of God out of Babylon. The writer of Revelation called the Christians of the first-century catacombs away from the idolatrous seduction of empire with these provocative words:

> Fallen, fallen is Babylon the great!
> It has become a dwelling place of demons,
> a haunt of every foul spirit,
> a haunt of every foul bird,
> a haunt of every foul and hateful beast.
> For all the nations have drunk
> of the wine of her fornication,
> and the kings of the earth have committed fornication with her,
> and the merchants of the earth have grown rich from the power
>   of her luxury. ...
> Come out of her, my people,
> so that you do not partake in her sins,
> and so that you do not share in her plagues;
> for her sins are heaped high as heaven,
> and God has remembered her iniquities.[2]

John of Patmos knew that for Christians living in the Roman Empire, faithfulness to Jesus meant they had to be deeply, even dangerously, countercultural. There was simply no way for a first-century Christian to be comfortable with Rome *and* faithful to Jesus. You had to choose one or the other. In the Jesus Movement of the 1970s—though we didn't know how to properly read Revelation as a prophetic critique of the Roman Empire (and thus a prophetic critique of all empires)—we did know that following the Lamb required us to be countercultural Christians. When we said, "One Way!" (the rallying slogan of the Jesus Movement), we meant that Jesus was the only way to life, and we instinctively knew that it was incompatible with the American way of materialism, militarism, and individualism. And so we joyfully embraced a faith that was bracingly countercultural.

But we were so very young.

As it turned out most of us were not very well equipped to resist the gradual slide toward the materialism of the prosperity gospel, the militarism of the religious right, and the individualism of American evangelicalism. In time, most of us ceased to be countercultural Christians and instead became conventional conservative Americans with a Jesus fish on our SUVs.

Through my teens and twenties I was happy to remain a counterculture "Jesus freak." I knew that following Jesus required me to resist the dominant culture of materialism and militarism. But eventually the Jesus Movement was absorbed by the Charismatic Movement and would be slowly seduced by the siren songs coming from the prosperity gospel and the religious right. The gradual synthesis of the gospel with material prosperity and political power happened gradually enough, and with enough biblical proof-texting, to make it seem plausible. And I went along for the ride.

I went along for the ride because I had been lulled to sleep, but in my mid-forties I suddenly woke up. An alarm clock had gone off in my soul. In an astonishing way, I realized I was tangled up in red, white, and blue. Awakened and disturbed at how comfortable American Christianity had become with the dominant culture, I thought, "How did we get here?" It's like we got on the wrong bus somewhere back down the line. We didn't start out as radical followers of Jesus only to end up being duped by a cadre of prosperity gospel hucksters and religious right power-mongers! So I revolted and rediscovered (at great cost) the counterculture faith I first knew as a teenager. My journey away from the compromised faith of Americanism and into the richer and more radical faith I embrace today is the story I tell in my books *A Farewell To Mars* and *Water To Wine*. Though the road back home was sometimes painful, I've never once regretted my decision to return to the radical roots of a counterculture Christianity. It was a decision that saved my soul. It was a costly decision, but like the pearl of great price, it was worth it.

The original name for what would eventually become known as Christianity was "the Way." You won't find the term "Christianity" in the Bible, but you will find "the Way" seven times in the book of Acts. If you had asked a follower of Jesus during the first century, "What's your religion?" she most likely would have replied, "I belong to the Way." This is what the Apostle Paul said in his hearing before the Roman governor Felix: "I admit that I follow the Way, which they call a cult."[3] The earliest believers' shared life of following Jesus together was called the Way, not because it was the way to heaven (the afterlife was never the emphasis), but because they had come to believe that following Jesus was the new and true way to be human. And because the lifestyle of the Way was such a radical departure from the way of the Roman Empire, it's no surprise that people viewed the Way with great suspicion and often derided it as a cult.

And there is a sense in which the Way *was* a cult—not in the abusive or heretical way we often use the word, but in its more technical sense. Literally, a cult is a system of religious devotion directed toward a particular figure. It's worth noting that the word *culture* comes from *cult*. Culture is derived from how and what people worship. Anthropologically speaking, religion and culture are nearly synonymous. Much of the drama we find in the book of Acts is the result of the inevitable clash between competing cults/cultures. At the same time that the cult(ure) of Caesar was emerging in the eastern provinces of the Roman Empire, the cult(ure) of Jesus was taking root in many of the same places. The book of Revelation is the attempt of John of Patmos to inspire fidelity to Christ among believers who are facing the powerful seductions of the emperor cult. Many citizens of the Roman Empire directed their devotion to Rome through the veneration of the emperor. The cult of emperor worship was really just a way of personifying empire worship. The veneration of Caesar was mostly viewed as a patriotic gesture. To place a dash of incense in a censor before a bust of Caesar in the marketplace was not much different than saluting the flag or placing your hand on your heart for the National Anthem. It was a seemingly innocuous gesture that actually carried deep symbolic meaning.

The most radical thing about the early Christians wasn't that they worshiped Jesus as God—the Greco-Roman world was awash in gods. Indeed, from the very beginning Christians *did* believe that Jesus was God, but the radical and dangerous thing about them was that they worshiped Jesus as *emperor!* This is what they meant when they confessed, "Jesus is Lord." The titles "Son of God," "King of Kings," "Savior of the World," "Prince of Peace," and "Lord of All" were already in circulation as imperial titles on Roman coins when the Christians began re-appropriating them in their worship of a Galilean Jew who had been crucified by a Roman governor. This was dangerous. This is why from time to time bishops were hauled before Roman magistrates, and some Christians ended up facing gladiators and wild beasts in the arena. It wasn't the *religion* of the Christians that got them in trouble per se, but the *political implications* of their religion. Because the Christians belonged to a different cult than the Roman Empire, they developed a different culture and became a counterculture movement—a counterculture that the authorities sometimes deemed threatening and periodically sought to violently suppress.

Because the early Christians refused to venerate Rome and the emperor in even benign and symbolic ways, they were viewed as unpatriotic. This was the impetus for the persecution of Christians. So it might be expected that there would be times when some Christians would try to accommodate their faith to the patriotic impulses of the empire. When some Christians in Asia Minor during the reign of Caesar Domitian began to view the symbolic veneration of the emperor as harmless, John of Patmos warned of the peril of those who have the mark of the beast upon their head or hand. The Revelator is desperate to remind the seven churches in Asia Minor that even when the emperor is seemingly humane and tolerant, the empire at its heart remains a beast, as typified by Caesar Nero (the number of whose name is 666!).

The original Jesus movement was not a pietistic religion of private belief about how to go to heaven when you die. The original Jesus movement was a countercultural way of public life. It was the kingdom of Christ, and as such it was a rival to the kingdom of Caesar. This is what made the principalities and powers of Rome so nervous about the Way. Though it's well known, it still needs to be emphasized that Jesus and his two most important apostles, Peter and Paul, were all executed by the Roman Empire. Why? Not for their religious beliefs about an afterlife, but because the kingdom of heaven they announced and enacted posed a challenge to the dominant myth that Rome had a manifest destiny to rule the nations and a divine right to shape history. Either it was Jesus who was the last best hope of the earth or it was Rome. But it couldn't be both.

If Christianity is not seen as countercultural and even subversive within a military-economic superpower, you can be sure it is a deeply compromised Christianity. A Christianity at home in an empire is the kind of compromised Christianity that the book of Revelation so passionately and creatively warns us against. A church in bed with a superpower is what Constantine inaugurated when he believed that Christ and Roma could be wed. But Christ cannot be wed to Roma. Christ can only be wed to his bride, the church. The reality is that the goddess Roma—who John rudely calls "Babylon the great, mother of whores"[4]—is never wed to Christ but rides the back of the Beast to her inevitable demise. For all its promises of peace and security, there is no salvation in the Beast. The baptized have placed all of their faith in the Lamb; even if those who are true to Jesus are vilified for their faith and become fodder for lethal entertainment in the Coliseum, the truth remains—"The kingdom of the world has become the kingdom of our Lord and of his Messiah, and he will reign forever and ever."[5]

Today as I call Christians to the practices of radical forgiveness and nonviolent peacemaking that Jesus embodies and most clearly sets forth in the Sermon on the Mount and that was the accepted practice of the early church, I often encounter Christians using Romans 13 as a kind of rebuttal. (Though whom they're rebutting—me or Jesus—isn't always clear.) Their argument generally goes something like, "God has ordained the government and has given it the sword to execute vengeance, therefore we cannot be opposed to war because Romans 13 sanctions 'Just War.'" Usually this argument is given to me in the context of advocating that the United States government should wage total war on Islamic terrorist organizations and other enemies of America. Their position is that the church should support and even celebrate this. But this is an egregious misinterpretation and misapplication of what Paul is talking about.

First of all, are we really comfortable with using Paul to trump Jesus? *That **is** what's being done!* Why is it that we are so prone to interpret Jesus in the light of a particular reading of Paul? (A reading of Paul that I—and many others—would argue is a conditioned *misreading* of Paul.) Why not take the Sermon on the Mount at face value and insist that any interpretation of Paul must line up with Jesus? Why not center our reading of Scripture with Jesus? I'm quite sure Paul would be entirely happy with this approach!

So let's start with this: Romans 13 is *not* the place to start! You cannot divorce Romans 13 from the clear context of Romans 12. (The arbitrary choice for the chapter break was unfortunate and has contributed to the problem.) In Romans 12, Paul is obviously drawing upon the Sermon on the Mount as he calls Christians in Rome to bless those who persecute them, to refuse retaliation, to act charitably toward enemies, and to overcome evil with good. In Romans 12, Paul is speaking directly to the believers in Rome, using the pronoun "you." But when Paul talks about Caesar in Romans 13, the pronoun changes to "he." To put it bluntly, Romans 13 isn't about you—Romans *12* is about you! Regardless of what Caesar might do with the sword of vengeance, and however we might envision God accomplishing sovereign purposes through a pagan government, followers of Jesus are called to renounce revenge and love their enemies. Always. This is the Jesus way.

What Paul is doing in Romans 13 is calling Christians living in the Roman Empire to obey civil laws and not be drawn into violent revolutionary movements. Paul understands that the kingdom of Christ is never established by violence and the Roman Empire cannot be converted to Christ by violence. What Paul seems to be commending in Romans 13 is what we might describe as police function. The empire as night watchman. We should recognize an important distinction between police function and the waging of war. Even though at times the line of distinction can be blurred, there really is an important difference between the two. We should recognize there *is* an enormous distinction between the town constable arresting a burglar and the bombing of Hiroshima!

I'm committed to Christian nonviolence, but I'm not an anarchist. I view police function as necessary to maintain a civil society. But no matter what I think about it, it's clear that Paul does *not* envision Christians possessing Caesar's sword. From Paul's perspective, this was simply impossible. When Paul talks about the government in Romans 13, he is talking about a pagan government in rebellion to the Lordship of the resurrected and ascended Christ. But the pagan government still serves a useful purpose in maintaining a civil society. What Paul is *not* thinking is that he's giving Christians a way to ignore Jesus and the Sermon on the Mount!

It seems that Paul's biggest concern in this passage is to call Jewish believers in Rome away from participation in violent revolution against the empire. Paul is writing his epistle to the Romans about a decade before the outbreak of the First Jewish War—a catastrophe that ended in hundreds of thousands of Jewish deaths and the destruction of Jerusalem. Paul was very aware of the yearning for violent revolution fomenting in Jerusalem and didn't want followers of Jesus in Rome to be infected with this contagion. Just as Jesus warned of the impending disaster that awaited Jerusalem if they rejected the things that make for peace as he wept over the city,[6] so Paul wants to warn believers in Rome against adopting romantic notions about violent revolution against the empire. As Paul says, Caesar "does not bear the sword in vain."[7]

If we had asked Paul, "but what happens when the emperor becomes a Christian?"—I think Paul would have been incredulous, saying, "that could never happen." But it did happen. Sort of. And that's where the mess really begins—with a quasi-Christian emperor. I say, "quasi-Christian," because even Constantine himself apparently understood that he could not be a Christian *and* be emperor *at the same time.* This could explain why Constantine delayed being baptized for twenty-four years until he was on his deathbed.

In any case, after Constantine, Romans 13 does begin to be employed by theologians as a way to call Christians to support the various war efforts of their Christian kingdoms and nations.

Until the Nazis.

Then what do we say? Should Christians in Nazi Germany have dutifully supported Hitler and his blitzkriegs by citing Romans 13? (By the way, they did!) No, obviously something has gone wrong. Sure, the idea of government-operated police function can be part of God's purposes to maintain a civil society where criminals—whether they are pagans or Christians—are apprehended and punished. But when we reach the point where Romans 13 is used to teach German Christians that supporting Hitler is their Christian duty, we know that this interpretation of Romans 13 has gone off its Christian rails!

It's not simply a matter of determining when Caesar has stepped over the line. That would be endlessly debated. Rather, it's a matter of understanding that though Caesar may serve a beneficial role as the town constable, Christians will never join with Caesar in waging war. In other words, the problem wasn't that the Third Reich arrested shoplifters, but that in the name of national destiny and self-defense it waged war on its European neighbors and tried to exterminate all of European Jewry.

So this is my question to American Christians who are fond of using Romans 13 to call for endless military buildup and waging what can only be an endless "war on terror." Why are the American Revolutionaries of 1776 exempt from Romans 13? Shouldn't they have been "subject to the governing authorities"[8] as Paul says? Is the use of Romans 13 to call for Christian support of American waging of war principled and consistent, or is it self-serving and inconsistent? Are we using Romans 13 to help clarify how Christians should live as "exiles" within an empire, or are we using Romans 13 to endorse the militarism of our favored empire?

What is obvious is that we should never pretend that Romans 13 is the only passage in Scripture that alludes to government. *Far from it!* Throughout Scripture the principalities and powers that govern the nations are more often cast in a very dark light. Whether it's Pharaoh in Exodus, Nebuchadnezzar in Jeremiah, the beastly empires in Daniel, or the Roman Empire as depicted in Revelation—these governments are not blithely commended but prophetically critiqued. And we should never forget that the man who wrote Romans 13 was executed by the government for not submitting to the governing authorities out of fidelity to Christ!

So, yes, Paul calls us to be "subject to the governing authorities." But let's not read into that more than we should. Jesus was subject to the governing authority of Pontius Pilate, but that doesn't mean the Roman governor was acting justly! On Good Friday the Roman government wasn't the servant of God—the Roman government was the servant of the satan! At his trial Jesus explained to Pilate that his kingdom was such that it forbade his followers to fight.[9] Jesus was subject to Rome in that he did not violently resist it—as Peter was so eager to do when he swung his sword against the arresting officers in Gethsemane. Jesus was "subject to the governing authorities," but in doing so he shamed the principalities and powers in his crucifixion and was vindicated by God in his resurrection. This is the posture toward evil that followers of Jesus are called to imitate. To pit Paul and Romans 13 against Jesus and the Sermon on the Mount is bad hermeneutics …and even worse Christianity.

So with a benign ambivalence we recognize that Caesar will resort to the sword, and when Caesar as constable keeps the criminals off the streets we can call it a service well rendered. But we are not followers of Caesar; we are followers of Christ. And even if the Beast can bring about a kind of order amidst chaos with his sword, for the Christian it doesn't really matter—we are followers of the slaughtered and victorious Lamb. We are called to "overcome evil with good"[10] and imitate those who "did not cling to life even in the face of death."[11]

The Christian is countercultural not just in opposition to the powers that be—for opposition can easily adopt the violent means that both Jesus and Paul condemned—but in opposition to violent power altogether. The sword is never really countercultural, but the cross always is. To follow Jesus and the way he taught, especially when living as a citizen of a military-economic superpower, is to be radically countercultural. The ways and values of superpowers are incompatible with the ways and values commanded by Jesus. Any serious attempt to live out the Sermon on the Mount in the context of a superpower will cause you to be viewed by the majority as a freakish outlier—a Jesus freak, if you will. The Jesus way, when truly lived, has always been viewed with suspicion by people in power. So be it. As the Apostle Paul said to the Roman governor, "I admit that I follow the Way which they call a cult." But Paul knew, as we do too, that it's the way to life.

The project of Christendom—trying to "Christianize" the world through complicity with Caesar—has come to an end. Secularism has triumphed over Christendom. This is obvious in Europe and is becoming increasingly apparent in North America. The Religious Right may not know this yet, but it will soon enough. Christendom is dead…but Christ is risen. What may appear to some Christians as a loss is actually an opportunity for the church to return to its radical roots. Tying the gospel to the interests of empire had a deeply compromising effect upon the gospel, as seen in the sordid history of the church being mixed up with imperial conquest, colonialism, and military adventurism around the world. If secularism helps bring that to an end, I can only say, hallelujah!

Those who lament the collapse of Christendom are like the two disciples on the Emmaus Road. They were depressed because Jesus had not turned out to be the kind of Messiah they anticipated. These disillusioned disciples (like everyone else who harbored hopes for a coming Messiah) assumed that Messiah would act according to the model of King David or Judah Maccabee, that he would be a militant revolutionary who would lead Israel in a violent revolt against Rome. After the events of Good Friday, the Emmaus Road disciples could only interpret the crucifixion of Jesus as the dismal failure of all they had hoped for. It took an encounter with the risen Jesus to open their eyes to the truth that Christ would not bring the kingdom of God with a slashing sword on a battlefield but with blessed and broken bread on the Communion table. Those lamenting the end of Christendom are grieving over what was a mistaken idea all along. The kingdom of God does not come through political force and cultural dominance but through the counter-imperial practices of baptism and Eucharist. With the end of Christendom we are forced to understand that Christ will not be with us as a conventional conqueror like Constantine or Charlemagne, but as the slaughtered Lamb providing the sacramental meal. If the world is to be changed by the gospel of Christ, it will not be changed on the battlefield or at the ballot-booth, but at the Communion table where sinners are offered the body and blood of Jesus in the form of bread and wine. The failure of Christendom is a blessed failure if it reminds us that we never needed the sword anyway—all we ever needed were the sacraments. We need the water of baptism. We need the bread and wine of Communion. We never needed the sword of political power.

It's not the task of the church to "Make America Great Again." The contemporary task of the church is to make Christianity countercultural again. And once we untether Jesus from the interests of empire, we begin to see just how countercultural and radical Jesus' ideas actually are. Enemies? Love them. Violence? Renounce it. Money? Share it. Foreigners? Welcome them. Sinners? Forgive them. These are the kind of radical ideas that will always be opposed by the principalities and powers, but which the followers of Jesus are called to embrace, announce, and enact. And the degree to which the church is faithful to Jesus and his radical ideas is the degree to which the church embodies a faith that is truly countercultural. It's not the Christianity of Constantine that can face the challenge of secularism, but the Christianity of the catacombs.

CHAPTER 2

A CAMINO OF CRUCIFIXES

The dripping blood our only drink,
The bloody flesh our only food:
In spite of which we like to think
That we are sound, substantial flesh and blood—
Again, in spite of that, we call this Friday good.
—T.S. Eliot, Four Quartets

During the final weeks of the 2012 Presidential campaign (Barack Obama versus Mitt Romney) I told my wife, Peri, I couldn't bear to be in America for the final throes of another Presidential election season. The acrimony of partisan politics, the madness of 24-7 news coverage, the fevered pitch of religious fanaticism that claimed God was on one side or the other—all of this was beyond the pale and more than I could endure. So I told Peri we would need to be out of the country in the fall of 2016. For the wellbeing of our souls we would put an ocean between us and the quadrennial insanity of American politics. Sometimes it takes an ocean not to break. Four years in advance, we decided we would take our first sabbatical after thirty-five years of full-time ministry. We would do it during September and October of 2016. This is clearly one of the most prescient decisions I've ever made! Little did we know that in 2016 presidential politics would reach unprecedented heights of lunacy and hostility! It was Peri who suggested that during our sabbatical escape from America we should walk the Camino de Santiago—a five-hundred-mile medieval pilgrim route from St.-Jean-Pied-de-Port, France to Santiago de Compostela, Spain. I enthusiastically agreed with her excellent idea, and so that's what we did. In the fall of 2016 while Trump and Clinton engaged in Mixed Martial Arts Politics, we disconnected and trekked across Northern Spain on the Camino de Santiago. As far as I'm concerned, it's the best thing we've ever done! The peace that slowly seeped into my soul during our long walk is still with me today. (Peri tells the story of our experience on the Camino in her memoir, *Every Scene by Heart*.)

We began our Camino on September 14—Holy Cross Day on the church calendar. The first segment of the Camino is a strenuous hike across the Pyrenees from St.-Jean in France to Roncesvalles in Spain. After arriving in Roncesvalles, I stepped into a thirteenth-century chapel next to the monastery's hostel where we were staying. As my eyes adjusted to the dim light typical of Romanesque chapels, my attention was drawn to the crucifix. I sat on a bench resting from the long hike over the Pyrenees gazing at the crucifix and sensed the Holy Spirit giving me instructions for my five-hundred-mile walk. The heavenly spiritual director seemed to say,

> Enter every church you can.
> Pay attention to every crucifix you see.
> Ask this question: What does this mean?
> Don't be too quick to give an answer.

And that's what I did. Every day. For forty days. Five hundred miles. All across Spain. My Camino was a camino of crucifixes. My Camino was a forty-day meditation on Christ crucified. Sometimes I would stand just inside the door of the church and look at the crucifix for a few moments. Other times I would remove my pack and sit in front of a crucifix for half an hour, always asking the question, what does this mean, but heeding the admonition to resist giving a quick explanation. I was being invited to venture deeper into the mystery of Christ crucified. Day after day I carried the images of these crucifixes in my heart and mind with plenty of time to meditate on the meaning of Good Friday during our five or six-hour hikes.

Midway through our Camino, we took our only rest day. We were in the province of Palencia and stayed two nights in the village of Frómista to recover from blisters and fatigue. During our rest day in Frómista, I visited the thousand-year-old Church of San Martin three times. I was usually the only person there. I prayed through my morning liturgy of prayer. I sat with Jesus. I contemplated the crucifix. I tried to imagine the worshipers who gathered in this church a thousand years ago. Why did they come? They didn't come to hear a motivational talk or a "practical" sermon; they didn't come to hear a praise band. They came because it was a sacred place where the sacraments were present. These medieval worshippers inhabited a world that was imbued with the sacred. Sadly, we no longer live in that world but a secular world where the sacred has been almost entirely banished. Sitting in the thousand-year-old church I wrote these words in my journal: "Once the sacred has been lost to the wrecking ball of secularism, can it be recovered? If yes, how? If no, what now?" Of course I'm enough of a modern man to acknowledge that much of the pre-modern sense of the sacred was mixed with superstition—superstition that was often used as a means of manipulating the credulous masses. I don't have an overly romantic attachment to the pre-modern period. Still I can't help but view the loss of the sacred in modernity as a forlorn tragedy.

> Disillusioned words like bullets bark
> As human gods aim for their mark
> Make everything from toy guns that spark
> To flesh colored Christs that glow in the dark
> It's easy to see without looking too far
> That not much is really sacred[1]

Not much is really sacred. That's true. But there I was gazing upon a crucifix as I sat in a church that had been built midway between Good Friday and just another Monday in late modernity. That crucifix was sacred, wasn't it? I knew it was. The crucifix was a life-size wooden sculpture depicting the defining moment in the story of Jesus of Nazareth. Jesus' hands and feet were nailed to a cross. His head was bowed in surrender, his eyes closed, his face tranquil. The artist had painted streams of blood flowing from the wounds in his head, hands, side, and feet. Yet the effect wasn't garish but serene. This crucifix conveyed peace to me. How odd that is! After all, a crucifix is on one level the graphic portrayal of a man being tortured to death. And yet it's also the very heart of the good news. This is the mystery of the gospel.

As the Spirit had directed me, I paid close attention to the crucifix, asking the question, "What does this mean?" and not being too quick to give an answer. Trite and tidy answers about the meaning of Good Friday are how we domesticate the cross. This is the bane of atonement theories. Instead of the crucifixion remaining the pivotal event in a compelling story, it's turned into a sterile formula. The cross is diminished to one of the Four Spiritual Laws or a waypoint on the Roman Road. This is how the cross is sanitized and made mechanical. The storyline is lost and the scandal is swept aside.

I'm not sure why Protestants abandoned crucifixes for empty crosses, but I think it was a mistake. I know that Protestants often argue that Jesus didn't remain on the cross; but he didn't remain in the manger either, and Protestants don't seem to have an objection to Nativity scenes. The truth is, Jesus *was* crucified and this *is* the epicenter of the gospel. Paul tells the Galatians, "It was before your eyes that Jesus Christ was publicly portrayed as crucified."[2] A crucifix replaced with an abstract symbol removes the crucifixion from the story and seems to indicate a move to reduce the cross to a kind of mathematical sign or theological equation. This gives rise to pallid descriptions of the cross like, "God turning our minus into a plus." Once we do that we can easily lose sight of the scandal of the cross. And the cross *is* a scandal!

One of the most remarkable things about the earliest Christians is that they didn't try to hide, downplay, or gloss over the fact that the One they worshiped as King of Kings had been crucified. Paul says things like, "I decided to know nothing among you except Jesus Christ and him crucified."[3] The early Christian hymn that Paul quotes in his letter to the Philippian church doesn't merely say Jesus died but that he was crucified.[4] The earliest Christian creed doesn't flinch from confessing that Jesus suffered under Pontius Pilate and was crucified.

For Christians living at such a far remove from the first century the depth of this scandal may be hard to grasp, but the crucifixion of your hero would be the *last* thing a Jew or a Roman living in antiquity would boast about. And yet the early Christians *did* boast about it. Paul readily admitted that this was foolishness to Romans and offensive to Jews. But Paul also said it was the power and wisdom of God, contending that "God's weakness is stronger than human strength."[5] Paul doesn't mean that when God is weak, God is still stronger than humans. That wouldn't be scandalous but just a typical boast about conventional power. Rather Paul is saying that God's power *is* weakness! Think about that for a moment and you will realize that such an assertion is still scandalous today. We are fascinated by conventional power—power to purchase, power to enforce our will, power to kill—and we are put off by any form of powerlessness. But it is precisely the powerlessness of God enacted by Jesus on the cross that saves the world.

As I walked from church to church, from crucifix to crucifix for five hundred miles, always meditating on the incongruity of beholding beauty and saving power in the depiction of a crucified man, I couldn't help but be struck by the tragic folly engulfing the majority of white evangelicals on the other side of the Atlantic. Their absurd line of reasoning was that God was going to accomplish divine purposes through a morally bankrupt (and occasionally financially bankrupt) real-estate tycoon turned reality TV star. Just try following that logic while gazing for thirty minutes at a crucifix! If you hold to a merely abstract notion of the cross—especially one that draws upon economic metaphors—I suppose such absurdities might almost seem feasible. If you're still fascinated by worldly power, I can see how you might be enthralled by a bully. But if you actually meditate on a visible portrayal of Christ crucified, the notion of God working through the tawdry machinations of power politics appears as ludicrous as it is. But in Babylon, power trumps everything.

Whatever it means for the world to be saved, God does *not* do it through the worldly means of power involving politics, weapons, and war, but through the unconventional means of utter powerlessness— through the crucifixion of a Galilean Jew who preached the kingdom of God. Meditating on crucifixes every day for six weeks changed me. It drew me back into the scandalous center of the gospel. The gospel is not motivational talks about happy marriages, being debt free, and achieving your destiny. That all belongs to the broad world of proverbial wisdom. It's fine as far as it goes, but it has little or nothing to do with the gospel. The gospel is about the cross and the cross is about a scandal. The cross is a scandal because it involves shame. But who is shamed by the cross? Is it the naked man nailed to a tree or the principalities and powers who in their naked bid for power put him there? To answer this question honestly is to enter deeply into the scandal of the cross.

The crucifixion of Jesus is easily the most depicted event in human history. How many billions of crucifixes have been formed, fashioned, carved, and painted over the past two millennia? And yet what is it that is being depicted in these billions of crucifixes? On a purely objective level, it is the torture and execution of an innocent man at the hands of those who run the world by the means of violent power. The crucifixion is the damning indictment of the world as it has been arranged. What the cross tells us is that when the Son of God entered our world—the world created by Cain and all the kings who followed in his bloody wake—our systems of violent empire and sacrificial religion nailed him to a tree. This is the moment when the principalities and powers who run the world were put to open shame; their claim of being wise and just was shown to be nothing but an empty sham. What they called wisdom and justice was nothing more than a cheap disguise concealing their naked lust for wealth and power. Paul says the rulers and authorities were shamed by the triumphant truth-telling of the cross.[6] Every crucifix reminds us that our systems of civilization built around an axis of power enforced by violence are not to be trusted. The myths, monuments, anthems, and memorials of every empire are designed to cleverly hide the bodies of the weak who have been trodden down by the mighty in their march to "greatness." The cross is the unveiling. The cross is the great truth-telling. The cross is the guilty verdict handed down upon empire. The cross is the eternal monument to the Unknown Victim. Yes, the cross is where the world is forgiven, but not before the world is found guilty.

A Camino of crucifixes helped me perceive the great gulf between the peaceable kingdom of Christ and the bloody empires of Babylon.

That God entered into human history as a crucified victim and not as a crucifying punisher finally reveals the true relationship between God and violence—a relationship that is sometimes confusing in the pages of Scripture. Violence is so prominent in the Bible because violence is the problem the Bible must address. The Bible looks honestly and unflinchingly upon the world as it is, and thus the pages of Scripture often drip with blood. But using the violent passages of the Bible to justify or normalize violence is like using the Bible to endorse slavery. Of course both have been done. Colonial interpreters and imperial theologians can and have forced the Bible to serve a violent lie. But on Good Friday the truth is told, for at Golgotha we discover a God who would rather die than kill his enemies. A billion crucifixes have revealed God as nonviolent. To paraphrase Hans Urs von Balthasar, being disguised under the disfigurement of an ugly crucifixion and death, Christ upon the cross is paradoxically the clearest revelation of who God is. The violence of the cross is not what God does, the violence of the cross is what God endures. The cross is not what God inflicts upon Christ in order to forgive. This is what N.T. Wright has called a "paganized soteriology."[7] The cross is not the violent appeasement of a pagan deity, but what God in Christ suffers as God pardons the world. God does not employ and inflict violence; God absorbs and forgives violence. The cross is where God in Christ transforms the hideous violence of Good Friday into the healing peace of Easter Sunday. The silent witness of every crucifix bears testimony to this, though I sadly admit we have been very slow to learn this lesson; at times the church has forgotten it all together.

The origin of the Camino de Santiago in the ninth century is connected to various legends regarding Saint James (Santiago). All along the Camino, you'll find statues and paintings of Saint James. Often he is portrayed as a Camino pilgrim festooned with the garb and equipment of a medieval traveler. I love the image of Saint James as a wayfaring pilgrim. But Saint James of the Camino has an evil twin. When not depicted as a Camino pilgrim, Saint James is often depicted as Santiago Matamoros—Saint James the Moor-Slayer. In this version, Saint James is shown as a sword-wielding conqueror riding a warhorse while trampling and decapitating Moors. The hyper-violent image of Santiago Matamoros emerged during the centuries-long bloody conflict between Spanish Christians and North African Muslims. The temptation to imagine God on their side in the form of a war-waging saint trampling and decapitating their enemies was too much for most Spanish Christians to resist, and these gruesome images still haunt churches throughout Spain.

One of the major cities along the Camino is Burgos where we spent an afternoon exploring the enormous thirteenth-century cathedral with its twenty-one chapels. Though I enjoyed my afternoon of quiet contemplation in the cathedral, it was clear that the grand edifice was in part an architectural tribute to the power and wealth of the Spanish Empire. And that's the problem. The syncretism of the kingdom of heaven and violent empire that created Christendom has been a blight on the gospel since the fourth century. In one of the chapels in the Burgos Cathedral the suffering Christ and the murderous Matamoros are present in the same altarpiece. *In the same altarpiece!* In that chapel you can gaze simultaneously upon a suffering Savior forgiving his enemies and a warring saint killing his enemies. Did no one notice the stunning incongruence? I suppose we can call this an unwitting testament to the divided allegiances of Christendom. You can try to force Babylon and New Jerusalem into the same chapel, but in the end something has to give. Eventually we have to choose between a Christianity that looks like Christ crucified or a Christendom that looks like a sainted Moor-slayer. The church has a long history of trying to hold the two together, but eventually one will prevail over the other. We cannot serve God and Mammon, and we cannot serve God and Matamoros. Ultimately we must either pledge our allegiance to Christ the crucified or to Cortez the killer. The truth is, Santiago Matamoros has nothing in common with the martyr Saint James, but he has a lot in common with the conquistador Cortez.

Like most pilgrims on the Camino I got blisters and one blister during the middle of the Camino was especially dreadful. I walked on that cursed blister for two weeks! There were times during a twelve or thirteen-mile day that it was pure agony. In dark humor I dubbed it "a messenger of Satan to torment me."[8] Often when my feet were hurting and I walked into a church to meditate on the crucifix, my attention would be drawn to the pierced feet of Christ. Eventually I came to see my painful feet as a gift...even if it was a gift I really didn't want. My painful feet alerted me to the truth that Christ entered our world to share our sorrows and bear our pain, as the prophet Isaiah said about the messianic Suffering Servant, "He carried our pains."[9]

On the fourth of October, we passed through the town of Villacázar de Sirga and paid a quick visit to the thirteenth-century Templar church, Santa Maria La Virgen Blanca. In the church I found a painting of Christ crucified with this Latin inscription above it: *Dolores Nosotros Ipse Portavit* (He has borne our pains). I sat for a moment in the church and wrote this in my journal,

> "To walk this world is to walk in pain, but let us walk as the pardon of God. I've believed all along that God wants me to walk this Camino, and if I'm supposed to walk two hundred miles or more in pain, so be it. Jesus was a man of sorrow, acquainted with pain. So as I walk with pain I try to remember those I know who live with pain—physical, mental, emotional, spiritual pain. And I pray for them. 'By his wounds you have been healed.'[10] Here is a sacred mystery: When we bring our wounds to Christ, it does not increase woundedness, but tends toward healing."

The day after I wrote those words my feet began to heal, and a few days later my feet were blister-free. I walked the rest of the Camino without any pain; but the gift of pain had taught me a valuable lesson and for that I thank God. With every crucifix I encountered on the Camino I beheld the wounds of Christ venerated in sacred art. And why do we reverently memorialize the wounds of Christ? Because in the wounds of Christ we find the wound that heals the world.

When the Apostle Peter in the imperial capital wrote his first letter to the Christians living in the Asian provinces of the Roman Empire, he addressed them as strangers, foreigners, exiles, or resident aliens.[11] Peter uses this term for these new believers, not because they were actual foreigners, but because now that they had been baptized into Christ they had pledged their allegiance to a new kingdom and were to live as those no longer fully at home in the Roman Empire. The values of the Roman Empire orbited around the primacy of war and wealth, the military and the economy, Mars and Mammon. In empires obsessed with "greatness," armies and economies are always given cultic devotion. But with their baptism, these believers were now expatriates living in a foreign land; now they were to live as strangers to the ways and means of Rome. Peter opens his letter by calling its recipients foreigners and closes his letter by saying, "Your sister church here in Babylon sends you greetings."[12] This is Peter's cryptic way of telling Christians living in the provinces that Rome was not "a shining city upon a hill," but an idolatrous empire in rebellion to God. Rome was not the Eternal City, but Babylon…and Babylon is always falling.[13] Peter reminds Christians living in the Roman Empire that they are citizens of the heavenly Jerusalem living as resident aliens in a fallen Babylon, and they must not confuse their allegiance. (Later the writer of Revelation will take the prophetic motif of Rome as Babylon to new heights.)

In the second chapter of his letter Peter gives a poetic meditation on the cross as a way of contrasting the ways of Christ with the ways of Caesar (the anti-Christ).

> He never sinned,
> nor ever deceived anyone.
> He did not retaliate when he was insulted,
> nor threaten revenge when he suffered.
> He left his case in the hands of God,
> who always judges fairly.
> He personally carried our sins
> in his body on the cross
> so that we can be dead to sin
> and live for what is right.
> By his wounds
> you are healed.[14]

What a stark contrast between Christ and Caesar! Did Tiberius sin? Did Caligula deceive? Did Claudius retaliate? Did Nero threaten? What a ridiculous question! Of course they did! This is what Caesars always do, and they do it in the most grotesque and highhanded ways. But Christ did not. Christ did not sin or deceive or retaliate or threaten. And Christ is now the world's new and true emperor. Through faith and baptism, the converts to whom Peter is writing now belong to the empire of Christ so Peter tells them, "He is your example, and you must follow in his steps."[15] In a world that admires men of power and wealth, supremely exemplified in the Caesars and their modern equivalents, Christians are to follow the example of a poor and humble Galilean who was crucified by a Roman governor. No wonder Peter speaks of Christians as exiles! The ways of empire are to be utterly foreign to those who worship and follow Jesus of Nazareth. The priorities of a superpower will inevitably be the antithesis of those found in the Sermon on the Mount.

For the first three hundred years of the church any suggestion that the aims of the kingdom of Christ could be served by corrupt Caesars would have been viewed as ludicrous or even demonic. The early Christians knew that the ways of Jesus and the ways of Caesar are forever incompatible. One is Christ; the other is anti-Christ. Though Christians prayed for Caesar to behave benignly, they always knew that Caesar was more likely to behave beastly. Empire is always bloody in tooth and claw. Christians never thought Caesar was capable of carrying out the work of Christ. Caesar advances the interests of the principalities and powers by wounding and killing the weak. Christ advances his kingdom by being a lamb wounded and killed. Peter could never have imagined a day when Christians would clamor over who should hold Caesar's bloody sword. Having made explicit the radical difference between the way of Christ and the way of Caesar, Peter then says something that is as mysterious as it is beautiful: "By his wounds you are healed."

In our wounded world abuse has a way of replicating itself so that it spreads like a virus. We all know that the abused often become abusers and that hurt people often end up hurting other people. Woundedness begets woundedness. This is especially true in the highly volatile realm of violence. Violence is a contagion that with its spread and inevitable escalation creates its own perverse logic; it's the logic of terrorism. We've all wondered how a terrorist can inflict such murderous cruelty on innocent people. But the terrorist has his logic. The terrorist will defend his actions by citing past abuses his people have suffered, and in the mind of the terrorist his means are justified by the ends he believes will be good. The terrorist always sees his actions as a response to previous violence and perceives his actions as primarily defensive. René Girard says, "the fact that no one ever feels they are the aggressor is because everything is always reciprocal … *The aggressor has always already been attacked.*"[16] This is the defense that ISIS and Al-Qaeda give. And isn't this precisely how President Harry S. Truman justified dropping two atomic bombs on cities full of civilians? Truman's argument for killing 200,000 people was no more sophisticated than that we were attacked and atomic bombs brought a good end. The winners get their face minted on money and the losers get tried for war crimes, but it's all the same logic.

The contagion of violence drives the logic of expositional escalation until so many are dead it's exhausted for a time. But only for a time. This is what John the Revelator portrays with the four horseman of the Apocalypse.[17] The white horse of conquest is followed by the red horse of war (because people resent being conquered), followed by the black horse of famine (because war is the most senseless waste of resources), and the pale horse of Death is always the final wraith rider. The endless repetition of this cycle is what we sanitize as "world history." So when Jesus arrives in Jerusalem on Palm Sunday he rides a donkey, the colt of a donkey—anything but a horse! On Good Friday Jesus puts an end to the vicious cycle of retaliatory violence that has kept the world from healing. Again, Peter says it like this,

> When he was abused, he did not return abuse; when he suffered, he did not threaten; but he entrusted himself to the one who judges justly.[18]

In the body of Jesus the abuse virus did not replicate itself. In the body of Christ the abuse virus died. The blood of Jesus became the vaccine to cure our addiction to reciprocal abuse and retaliatory violence. Week after week we partake of the Eucharist so that we might be agents of healing in a wounded world. Christians are to be carriers of the new contagion of forgiveness. In a world where the capacity for retaliatory violence is nearly infinite, forgiveness is our only sane and saving option. In a world of conflict every side sees the righteousness of their own cause, but the only righteousness that can save the world is the righteousness that imitates Christ in forgiveness.

> He himself bore our sins in his body on the cross, so that, free from our sins, we might live for righteousness; by his wounds you have been healed.[19]

On Good Friday a world deeply wounded by violence and vengeance sinned its sins into the body of Jesus and hung him upon a tree. Indeed Jesus bore our sins. What does the sin of the world look like? It looks like the lynching of an innocent victim. It looks like a crucifix. All the sins that mutate out of pride and blame, greed and violence, were sinned into the body of Jesus. But in the body of Jesus the abuse virus did not replicate itself; instead the body of Jesus became a grave for sin. Jesus took the sin of the world all the way down into death…and left it there. What does the salvation of the world look like? It looks like a crucifix. In his resurrection Jesus speaks peace to his disciples and commissions them to flood the world with his forgiveness. But even in his resurrection Jesus still wears his wounds, because, "by his wounds you have been healed." The sin of the world—in which we are all implicated to one degree or another—left its mark on Jesus. The wounds in Jesus' hands, feet, and side are the entry wounds of sin. But once sin entered into the body of Christ, *sin itself died!* Jesus took the virus of sin and transformed it into the remedy of forgiveness. This is the gospel of forgiveness.

Sin wounds us all—both the sinner and the sinned against. Do you think that ultimately the terrorist is any less wounded by his actions than those he wounds? Every wound we inflict upon another we also inflict upon our own soul. When Raskolnikov finally confessed his murders to Sonya in Dostoevsky's *Crime and Punishment*, her first response was, "What have you done to yourself!"[20] This is how sin works. Sin always carries its own punishment. Sin is a self-inflicted wound upon our soul, but by the wounds of Jesus we are healed. When we bring our wounds to Christ and lay them upon his wounds, healing begins. When the wounded Christ upon the cross prayed, "Father, forgive them," healing was released into the woundedness of the world.

It's not yet another war that will heal the world, but the wounds of Christ. Calvary was the last battlefield that made any sense. After Calvary, every other battlefield is a failure to understand that the ways of Cain and Caesar, the ways of war and greed, all died in the body of Christ on Good Friday. So now when we are wounded, we don't lash out at our adversary, we don't retaliate and replicate the virus; instead we forgive our brother-enemy and bring our wounds to the healing wounds of Christ. The body of Christ is where sin goes to die. And we who have been baptized, have been baptized into the body of Christ. This is a great mystery, but the baptized now belong to the wound that heals the world.

As I walked from St.-Jean to Santiago in the fall of 2016 contemplating five hundred miles of crucifixes, I saw more clearly than ever before the folly of trying to change the world through the way of force. Whether it's a Caesar with Roman legions or a Commander-in-chief with nuclear codes, the way of Cain trying to enforce his will by killing his brother, whom he calls other and enemy, has forever been shamed by the cross of Christ. Babylon still believes the old lie, and that's why it's fallen. But those who rally around a crucified Savior gain the capacity to become something truly new and other. With that newness and otherness comes the possibility of embodying a healing presence in our wounded world. Where the church adopts the form of a crucifix there is hope for the world.

CHAPTER 3

TANGLED UP IN RED, WHITE, AND BLUE

I had returned home from conducting prayer schools in San Francisco and Ontario, Canada and was going through a pile of mail. One piece came from a major evangelical ministry whose stated mission is "to advance the gospel of Jesus and His Kingdom into the nations." I had financially supported this ministry in the past, and to thank me for my contributions and encourage my future support they included with their appeal letter a gift of seventy-five return address stickers with my name and address printed on them along with other decorative stickers. What struck me as odd was that all seventy-five stickers were patriotic and military themed, festooned with American flags, soaring eagles, and the Statue of Liberty; each sticker bore patriotic slogans like *God Bless America, Proud American, Proud To Be An American,* and *Let Freedom Ring.* Fourteen of the stickers said *God Bless Our Troops.* Also included was a tiny hymnal emblazoned with the ministry's motto "To Know Christ and to Make Him Known." But the dozen hymns were all patriotic anthems: *The Star Spangled Banner, God Bless America, My Country 'Tis of Thee, America the Beautiful, Battle Hymn of the Republic, The Pledge of Allegiance, Stars and Stripes Forever, This Is My Country, God Bless the USA, The Preamble to The Constitution, You're a Grand Old Flag,* and *Taps.* It's hard to understand what Lee Greenwood's lyric, "I'm proud to be an American where at least I know

I'm free" has to do with their stated mission "to advance the gospel of Jesus and His Kingdom into the nations." But that's the way it is in a land where so much of the church is tangled up in red, white, and blue.

Of course this is really nothing new. The church in every western power after Constantine has at some point succumbed to the Siren seduction of empire and has conflated Christianity and nationalism into a single syncretic religion. Rome, Byzantium, Russia, Spain, France, England, and Germany have all done it. Seventeen centuries ago the Roman church got tangled up in imperial purple. In the 1930s, the German evangelical church got tangled up in Nazi red and black. The Anglican church spent a long time tangled up in the Union Jack. Today the American evangelical church is tangled up in red, white, and blue. That this kind of entanglement has been a common failure of the church for centuries doesn't make it any less tragic.

When the church lacks the vision and courage to actually *be the church*, it abandons its high calling of proclaiming the Lordship of Jesus and panders to power, soliciting its services as the high priest of religious patriotism. When the church colludes with the principalities and powers, it can no longer prophetically challenge them. A church in bed with empire cannot credibly call the empire to repent. The loss of prophetic courage leads to a pathetic capitulation. As William Cavanaugh has said,

> "We need an ecclesiology that is robust enough to counter the powers that be, but humble enough not to reproduce the exclusions and pride of those powers. If the church is not in some way a countersign to the powers, then it simply opens the way for other allegiances—to the state or the market, especially—to take hold."[1]

Indeed other allegiances have taken hold, as seen with a Christian ministry committed to "advancing the gospel of Jesus and His Kingdom into the nations" simultaneously exhorting us to "Support Our Troops." And this is done without any apparent sense of contradiction, as if the American military was the martial wing of the church of Jesus Christ. But there *are* contradictions. To advance the gospel of Jesus and his peaceable kingdom is indeed the mission of the church, but the kingdom of Jesus does not have troops. The consistent attitude of the early church toward the vocation of waging war is reflected in the words of Saint Cyprian (200–258) when he said, "The hand that has held the Eucharist will not be sullied by the blood-stained sword."[2] So what exactly is meant when churches and Christian ministries confess the ubiquitous mantra "Support Our Troops"? How are Christians to understand the possessive determiner "our" in this slogan? The assumption is that there is a seamless fit between the military objectives of the United States and the mission objectives of the church of Jesus Christ, but that is an outlandish assumption and blatantly false! The beautiful feet of those who proclaim the gospel of peace are not shod in combat boots, and those who carry the cross of Christ into the world are not clutching M16s. When the case is made that it is the American military that defends Christian religious liberty, we should listen to the early Christian philosopher Lactantius (240–320) who said, "Religion must be defended not by killing but by dying, not by violence but by patience."[3] Sadly, we are no longer a patient church.

The church is the vanguard of the Prince of Peace—the community of the baptized who have already turned swords into plowshares. Jesus himself made this explicit when he told Pontius Pilate, "My kingdom is not from this world. If my kingdom were from this world, my followers would be fighting … But as it is, my kingdom is not from here."[4] In other words, the kingdom of Jesus does not come from the world of war where armies go forth to fight and kill. The Apostle Paul was echoing this when he wrote, "Our struggle is not against enemies of blood and flesh, but against the rulers, against the authorities, against the cosmic powers of this present darkness, against the spiritual forces of evil in the heavenly places."[5] Thus in the pre-Constantine church the Apostolic Tradition "forbade a catechumen or baptized believer from entering the legions, but permitted him, if attracted to the faith while in the legions, to stay there on one condition: 'Let him not kill.'"[6]

But the idea of waging peace by patience instead of waging war by violence has been lost where the church has been willingly conscripted into serving the nation's military agenda. War is the ultimate impatience. Instead of hearing Jesus tell Peter to put away his sword, a church with a superstitious reverence for armed combat imagines Jesus leading soldiers into battle—as a thousand Facebook memes attest. Whether it's crusaders with crosses on their shields, German soldiers with *Gott Mit Uns* on their belt buckles, or American evangelicals fawning over the film *American Sniper*, waging war and following Jesus have been combined in a way that seeks to erase the contradiction established by Christ himself.

Often this is done by equating combat deaths with Jesus' nonviolent sacrifice of love. At the Courthouse in Andrew County, Missouri, where my father served as judge, a new war monument was dedicated on Memorial Day, 2017. It included this inscription: "Greater love hath no man than this, that he lay down his life for his friends. John 15:15." The obvious implication is that Jesus' death at the hands of the Roman Empire is somehow similar to the death of American soldiers who are killed while prosecuting war. It's true that both deaths are sacrificial, but the nature of these sacrificial deaths is quite different. The failure to see the clear difference between Jesus sacrificing his life while forgiving his enemies on the cross and the sacrifice of a soldier slain while waging war on a battlefield is an indication of the degree to which a commitment to militarism has obscured the implications of the gospel. But when waging war is regarded as a religious sacrifice, such confusions abound.

I have vivid memories of Memorial Day growing up in Savannah, Missouri. The last Monday in May marked the end of the school year and the beginning of summer vacation. As such it is a fond memory. And on Memorial Day I always went with my dad to a ceremony held in the northeast corner of the town cemetery. This is where the war dead are buried. Each uniform grave was decorated with a small American flag. As a child in the 1960s, the freshest graves contained the bodies of young men who had returned from Vietnam in flag-draped coffins. Old men were there wearing faded and ill-fitting uniforms from the wars of yesteryear. There would be a speaker (some years it was my dad), a prayer offered by one of the town's clergy, the National Anthem played by the high school band, a twenty-one gun salute from the old men in their faded uniforms, and taps played by a trumpeter in the distance.

The occasion was somber and patriotic. And the theme of the prayers and speeches was always the same—it was the language of sacrifice. In civic religion, war is always publically remembered as an act of sacrifice. Public remembrances of war are deeply liturgical because war is memorialized as a sacrament within civic religion. Stanley Hauerwas has taught us that nationalism is a religion with war as its liturgy. The nature of war sacrifice in civic religion is that there must always be more sacrifices. Mars is an insatiable god. The sacrifices can be momentarily suspended (in what is falsely called "peacetime") but never permanently abolished. Because the previous sacrifices *must*, as the liturgy states, "not have been in vain," the day will come when more sacrifices must be offered upon the bloody altar of war. This is the dark truth of war remembrance liturgies. Yes, the dead are remembered, lamented, and honored, but also boys (and now perhaps girls) are reminded in these liturgies that the day may come when they will be called upon to add more blood to the altar of sacrifice—either by killing or being killed. The justification for the perpetuation of war sacrifice is simple: because the previous sacrifices must "not have been in vain." Indeed, the recurring creed in war memorial liturgies is "They did not die in vain." To vainly die in war is the worst thing that can happen within the civic religion of sacrifice, because a vain sacrifice is a failed sacrifice, and failed sacrifices threaten to unravel the social cohesion that sacrificial religion provides. The community can rally together in unity around a heroic sacrifice, but not around a failed sacrifice.

Wars waged and especially wars won have always been the most effective way to unite a populace. In times of war the tribe, the nation, the empire rally in unity around the common cause of waging war upon a common enemy. The war dead are remembered and honored as heroic sacrifices in vanquishing evil. Thus the slain soldiers did not die in vain—they died as noble sacrifices. So whether Johnny comes marching home again or Johnny is shipped home in a flag-draped coffin, as long as the war is won, the state is unified around effective sacrifices— sacrifices that will be honored on the days of remembrance. Of course, all of this is done innocently, with almost no awareness of the dark reality that sacrifice always demands more sacrifice. Those who gather for memorial services see themselves as remembering and honoring the previous sacrifices. And this can be commendable. There is no doubt that battlefields are often sites of heroic sacrifice. But what is not generally recognized is that they are also participating in a ritual for the preparation of future sacrifices. For sacrifice to not be in vain, the cycle of sacrifice must be perpetuated.

But sometimes the cycle of sacrifice *is* broken. The cycle of perpetual war sacrifice can be broken by a crushing defeat, as in the case of Germany and Japan in WWII. If the defeat is absolute enough, it *can* (though not necessarily) lead a new generation to profoundly rethink its relationship to war. For example, the Japanese Constitution outlaws war as a means of settling international disputes involving the state. In the case of Japan, profound loss led to profound rethinking.

In the case of America's bitter experience in the Vietnam War, the defeat was not absolute, but ambiguous. The American objectives in the war were obviously not realized—a unified Vietnam became a Communist country after all—but the defeat was ambiguous enough that the civic liturgists could still try to employ the sacrificial language of "They did not die in vain"—though exactly what the sacrifice of 58,000 American lives in Vietnam actually accomplished is not quite clear.

What *is* clear is that in terms of being a unifying sacrifice, the American experience in Vietnam was a failure. As the war drug on without a clear victory, and as much of the nation began to question if America was morally right in why and how it waged the war, that which is unutterable in civic sacrificial religion began to be spoken openly: "Our boys are dying in vain." In civic religion, this is blasphemy. And thus violent riots during the Vietnam War era wracked America as each side accused the other of sacrilege. The sacrifices of the Vietnam War, instead of being unifying, became divisive. In sacrificial religion, this is a failed sacrifice. The deep fragmentation from the failed sacrifices of the Vietnam War is still felt today and is what lies behind much of the right-left political divide. Interestingly, it was during the Vietnam War that the American de facto state church shifted from Mainline Protestantism (which often opposed the war) to conservative Evangelicalism (which unequivocally supported the war).

Following the debacle of the Vietnam War and the divisiveness it wrought, what is to be done to unify a fractured nation? One approach would be to go out and win a "good old-fashioned war." Of course, winning wars is not as easy as the myths would have us believe; besides that, we seem to be in an age of asymmetrical warfare where conventional victory and surrender do not apply. It's hard to imagine how something as vague as the "war on terror" can be won in any way that resembles winning WWII. When the nation-states of Germany and Japan surrendered, America celebrated V-E and V-J Day. But it's hard to imagine a V-T Day. And even if you are able to arrange a "good old-fashioned war" between two nation-states wearing uniforms and all, in an age where both sides are likely to have nuclear arsenals, it's hard to imagine anyone "winning." If we are committed to generating social unity through the civic religion of war sacrifice, we may very well be on the road to global annihilation.

So what is the role of the church in a world that careens toward catastrophic war? Is it to shout hurray for our side and assure the masters of war that God is with us? Of course not! It's this kind of hubris and folly that led to the calamity of millions of Christians killing one another in the name of national allegiance during the two world wars. If the church is to be an ambassador of the good news and an agent of healing in the world, the church is going to have to become serious about being something other than the high priest of religious nationalism. With so many churchgoers entangled in the tentacles of nationalism, it's time for the church to actually be the church. As Stanley Hauerwas has said in so many ways, it's the task of the church to make the world the world. And for the church to appear as distinct from the world—the world of war that Jesus told Pilate his kingdom does *not* come from—the church is going to have to face the fact that it cannot pledge its allegiance to both Caesar and Christ. As Jesus said, "no one can serve two masters."[7]

What about patriotism? Is it permissible for a Christian to be patriotic? Yes and no. It depends on what is meant by patriotism. If by patriotism we mean a benign pride of place that encourages civic duty and responsible citizenship, then patriotism poses no conflict with

Christian baptismal identity. But if by patriotism we mean religious devotion to nationalism at the expense of the wellbeing of other nations; if we mean a willingness to kill others (even other Christians) in the name of national allegiance; if we mean an uncritical support of political policies without regard to their justice, then patriotism is a repudiation of Christian baptismal identity. It is extraordinarily naive for a Christian to rule out categorically the possibility of any conflict between their national identity and their baptismal identity. But it's precisely this kind of naiveté that is on display every time a church flies an American flag above the so-called Christian flag. Or perhaps it's a bit of unintended truth-telling.

Flags are powerful symbols that have the capacity to evoke strong emotions—think of the passion connected with protests involving flag burning. In the world of symbol, flags are among the most revered signs. So when a church flies the American flag above the Christian flag, what is the message being communicated? How can it be anything other than that all allegiances—including allegiance to Christ—must be subordinate to a supreme national allegiance? This is what Caiaphas admitted when he confessed to Pilate, "We have no king but Caesar."[8] When the American flag is placed in supremacy over all other flags—including a flag intended to represent Christian faith—aren't we saying our faith is subordinate to our patriotism? Is there any other interpretation? And if you're inclined to argue that I'm making too much out of the mere arrangement of flags on a church lawn, try reversing them and see what happens! For the "America First" Christian it would create too much cognitive dissonance to actually admit that their loyalty to Christ is penultimate, trumped by their primary allegiance to America, but there are plenty of moments when the truth seeps out.

This is why on July 4, 2017 I wrote a kind of "Dear John" letter to America.

Dear America,

Happy Birthday. Today you're 241 years old. I've known you for almost a quarter of your life, so I know you well. You've always been my home. But lately I feel something has come between us; there's been some misunderstandings and I would like to clear the air.

First of all, I love you. Like I said, you're my home. I've been all over the world, but I've always come home to you. There's so much I admire about you. Your energy, your creativity, your entrepreneurial spirit. You invented the blues, jazz, and rock 'n' roll. You've led the world for most of a century in science and technology. You even put a man on the moon! You came up with the idea of preserving vast tracts of your natural beauty through the genius of National Parks. (Some have suggested this is your best idea and I agree.) You've given us great artists like Walt Whitman, Flannery O'Connor, and Bob Dylan. You provided refuge for great thinkers like Albert Einstein, Hannah Arendt, and Abraham Joshua Heschel. You opened your door to millions of immigrants from around the world—the poor looking for nothing more than safe haven and a new opportunity. You welcomed the Zahnds from Switzerland at the beginning of the last century. Indeed, you're at your best when you live up to the lofty ideals of Lady Liberty.

Give me your tired, your poor,
Your huddled masses yearning to breathe free,
The wretched refuse of your teeming shore.
Send these, the homeless, tempest-tost to me,
I lift my lamp beside the golden door!"

Yes, America, I love you...but not like *that*. Not in the way of supreme allegiance and unquestioned devotion. You see, my heart belongs to another. I'm a Christian and I confess that *Jesus* is Lord. The Savior of the world is the crucified and risen Son of God, not "We the People." The gospel is the story of Jesus, not the American story. I know your sixteenth President claimed that America was "the last best hope of earth" and nearly every president since has echoed this creed, but it's simply not true. The last best hope of earth is Jesus, not you.

Okay, brace yourself. I'm going to say some hard things.

Sometimes you embarrass yourself when you get drunk on hubris. At times you display an arrogance that borders on blasphemous. I'm talking about the kind of religious patriotism that makes you an idolatrous rival to my faith in Jesus Christ. Your capital city is filled with none-too-subtle religious iconography. Take for example *The Apotheosis of Washington* in the Capitol Rotunda that depicts George Washington seated on the throne of glory in heaven. Obviously you know that *apotheosis* means to "make a god of"—because that's clearly what you're attempting to do with Washington. You appropriated the Christian iconography of Christ ascended to heaven and replaced Jesus Christ with George Washington. Come on now! That's a bit much, wouldn't you say? Honored as the nation's first President, fine. But made a god?! Do you mean to suggest that America is a divine creation with heavenly authority to rule the nations? And if that's not what you mean, then what *do* you mean to indicate with *The Apotheosis of Washington* in the Capitol? And this is just one example. You know I could cite many others.

That's what I mean when I say I love you, but not like *that!* If I loved you like *that* I would betray my baptism. I am betrothed by faith and baptism to Christ alone and Christ can have no rivals. Jesus told his followers, "Whoever comes to me and does not hate father and mother...cannot be my disciple."[9] Obviously, Jesus doesn't want his disciples to actually *hate* their parents, but he *is* making a point about the requirement of unrivaled allegiance. So, America, when people accuse me of hating you, please know it isn't true. I don't hate you. But I can't allow you to rival my allegiance to Jesus. I can't put you first. I have vowed to seek first the kingdom of God and you'll just have to understand that.

Now that we're this far into our difficult conversation I feel like I have to say some other things. It's true that I love your energy, creativity, and entrepreneurial spirit. I love your amazing contributions to science and art. I love you because you're my home. But there are things I don't love about you. Here we go.

I know you hate to be reminded of what you call "the past," but the truth is it's not past and you need to be reminded of it whether you like it or not. I'm talking about your twin original sins. The brutal enslavement of Africans for the sake of "The Economy" and the ethnic-cleansing of this land's indigenous inhabitants. You seem willing to acknowledge the sin of slavery. (Though you still have a long, long way to go in righting the entrenched wrongs of racism.) But you appear incapable of acknowledging your other great sin—the sin of genocidal ethnic cleansing. You want to pretend it didn't happen and get mad when I bring it up. But you're going to have to face it. I don't know exactly how you can atone for this sin, but I do know that you have to face the ugly fact that you built your nation on stolen land atop buried bodies. In building your "shining city upon a hill" you became Cain. You killed your brother. You can receive the mercy of God as Cain did, but you have to be honest about what you did to Abel—the aboriginal people who first populated this land. America, you're my home, but my home is haunted by native ghosts.

So please try to be more humble. You don't have to be "Great Again." It's enough to be good. You don't have to be so obsessed with being "Number One." It's enough to be a moral citizen among the community of nations. You don't have to try to be "King of the World." Jesus already is! And your obsession with possessing the means to kill—

your trillion-dollar war machine, two thousand nukes, billion-dollar bombers, not to mention your 270 million privately owned guns!—scares me. Your money says, "In God We Trust," but your actions say, "In Gun We Trust." It reminds me of something ominous that Jesus said: "All who take the sword will perish by the sword."[10] Please think about it.

America, I'm one of your citizens, and I do love you. I'll seek the common good. I'll gladly pay my share to help provide for education, infrastructure, healthcare, emergency services, and everything else it takes to live in a civilized society. (I'd like for you to spend a lot less on bombs and killing machines, but I understand that's not up to me.) Yes, America, I do love you, but not like I love my Lord. Not like I love God. I cannot love you like that. I cannot pledge unconditional allegiance to you. What I can promise is to be a good citizen by attempting to love my neighbor as myself. That will have to be enough.

On the Fourth of July I cannot worship you with the liturgies of civic religion, but I'll gladly eat a hotdog in honor of your birthday and listen to some Johnny Cash. And better yet, I can pray that you would become more peaceable and just, more humble and kind.

America, you don't need to be great. May God bless you to be good.

With Affection,

Brian Zahnd

I've been a pastor going on four decades and I can tell you that the greatest challenge to making disciples of Jesus in the American context is that most people are already thoroughly discipled into the rival religion of Americanism. America is a profound complexity and as such it is many things. America is a nation, a culture, an empire, a religion. As a nation and culture, America is a mixed bag, but there is much that is inspiring and admirable. As an empire, it is a rival to the kingdom of God, and as a religion it is a false god inviting idolatry. I'm well aware that speaking of America as a rival religion is a hard truth for patriotic "God and Country" Christians to accept, but is it really a matter of dispute? America *is* a religion—a religion complete with creation myths, holy days, holy ground, founding fathers, canonized saints, canonical texts, revered hymns, hallowed temples, sanctified statues, liturgical gestures, and sacred liturgies. To dispute the sacrosanct nature of any of these things is to court controversy and contempt. (Ask Colin Kaepernick.) The attempt to reconcile Christianity and Americanism into a single religion is the kind of religious syncretism that most conservative Christians claim to be so alarmed about.

A few years ago, I was invited to speak on prayer at a Christian school on the National Day of Prayer (an observance established in 1952 during the Cold War Era). As you might have guessed I'm less than enthusiastic about the National Day of Prayer, mainly because of its tendency to turn into the Day of Nationalistic Prayer. I would rather we observe Ascension Day as a global day of prayer. Ironically these two days occasionally coincide, and it's telling that the American National Day of Prayer easily overshadows observing the Ascension of Christ to reign over all the nations. But despite my ambivalence toward the National Day of Prayer, it was less trouble for me to accept the invitation than to decline. The student assembly was held in the gymnasium, and before I spoke the students were to recite the Pledge of Allegiance and the Lord's Prayer. The Pledge of Allegiance came off without a hitch—every student recited it flawlessly, complete with a hand-over-heart liturgical gesture. But the Lord's Prayer was another story; in fact it was a bit of a fiasco. The students in this private Christian school *didn't know* the Lord's Prayer. So a student was pressed into service to read it so he could lead the student body through it line by line in "repeat after me" fashion. It was embarrassing. I turned to the faculty member assigned to host me saying, "It's not that this Protestant Christian school doesn't believe in liturgy, you just don't believe in *Christian* liturgy; your students know their *American* liturgy quite well."

It was a harsh assessment on my part, but the faculty member could only sheepishly agree.

Christians can and should be productive citizens within the particular nation they happen to have residence; they should pray for political leaders and pay their taxes; they can vote and participate in public service and contribute to the public good. But they should not labor under the delusion that *the nation itself* can be Christian. Only that which is baptized can be Christian, and you cannot baptize a nation-state. This was the misguided and now abandoned aspiration of Christendom. And in the American experiment the United States deliberately broke with the Christendom practice of claiming to be a Christian nation with a state church. It was America that pioneered the experiment of secular governance. America is not a Christian nation; it never was and never can be. The only institution that even has the possibility of being Christian is the church. When we confuse the nation with the church, it may not do any particular damage to the nation, but it will do irreparable harm to the church. When we reach for the sword of violent power, we let go of the cross of Christian discipleship. To be Christian implies an intentional attempt to imitate the one who would rather die than kill his enemies. Whatever it means to be Christian, it would clearly preclude maintaining a trillion-dollar war machine. I'm sure the Joint Chiefs of Staff would agree that you cannot run the Pentagon according to the Sermon on the Mount.

When we admit it's impossible to govern according to the Sermon on the Mount, we also admit it's impossible for a nation that maintains a nuclear arsenal to be Christian. To contend that America could not survive without nuclear arms is to make my point. The people of God are sustained by the Holy Spirit, not hydrogen bombs. We have no warrant to hope for a Christian nation (as we conceive of nations); it's enough to hope for a Christian *church*. Only that which is capable of embodying the Sermon on the Mount has the possibility of being Christian. Some have tried to lessen the demands of discipleship by adopting Luther's "Two Kingdoms" theology, but this only leads to divided loyalties and a compromised Christianity. How do you have two kingdoms without two kings? When you understand that Christ means king...well, you see the problem. What ends up happening is Christ being reduced to a "spiritual" king (whatever that is), while the state is made the real king. Let's just say that Luther's "Two Kingdoms" experiment did not end well in Germany.

Despite abundant testimony from church history that ecclesial entanglement in the agenda of empire always leads to a compromised Christian witness, much of the American church is resolute in being tangled up in red, white, and blue. Today religious nationalism (which is disturbingly connected with white nationalism) is on the rise. In such an environment the church faces a stark choice: Will we comport ourselves as pious promoters of religious nationalism, or will we summon the courage to act as a prophetic witness against the idolatry of nationalism? Will we remain tangled up in red, white, and blue, or will we lash ourselves to the cross of Christ and willingly endure whatever suffering that may demand of us? One of the most vital things an American Christian can do right now is resist the hijacking of Christian faith by American nationalism. We need to make it abundantly clear that "America First" is incompatible with a global church whose mission it is to announce and embody the kingdom of Christ. The Nicene Creed teaches us that the baptized are to confess that "we believe in one holy catholic and apostolic church," not in a compromised and nationalistic church. Now is not the time for gaudy star-spangled Christianity; now is the time to wash our robes in the blood of the Lamb so that we can live as citizens of New Jerusalem.

> So perhaps the best moral sense Christians can make of the story of Christendom now, from the vantage of its aftermath, is to recall that the gospel was never bound to the historical fate of any political or social order, but always claimed to enjoy a transcendence of all times and places. ... That being so, surely modern Christians should find some joy in being forced to remember that they are citizens of a kingdom not of this world, that here they have no enduring city, and that they are called to live as strangers and pilgrims on the earth.[11]
>
> —David Bentley Hart

My Problem With the Bible

I have a problem with the Bible. Here's my problem…
I'm an ancient Egyptian. I'm a comfortable Babylonian.
I'm a Roman in his villa.

That's my problem. See, I'm trying to read the Bible for
all it's worth, but I'm not a Hebrew slave suffering in Egypt.
I'm not a conquered Judean deported to Babylon. I'm not a
first-century Jew living under Roman occupation.

I'm a citizen of a superpower. I was born among the
conquerors. I live in the empire. But I want to read the
Bible and think it's talking to me. This is a problem.

One of the most remarkable things about the Bible is
that in it we find the narrative told from the perspective of
the poor, the oppressed, the enslaved, the conquered, the
occupied, the defeated. This is what makes it prophetic.
We know that history is written by the winners. This is
true—except in the case of the Bible it's the opposite! This
is the subversive genius of the Hebrew prophets. They
wrote from a bottom-up perspective.

Imagine a history of colonial America written by
Cherokee Indians and African slaves. That would be a
different way of telling the story! And that's what the Bible
does. It's the story of Egypt told by the slaves. The story of
Babylon told by the exiles. The story of Rome told by the
occupied. What about those brief moments when Israel
appeared to be on top? In those cases the prophets told
Israel's story from the perspective of the peasant poor as a
critique of the royal elite. Like when Amos denounced the
wives of the Israelite aristocracy as "the fat cows of Bashan."

Every story is told from a vantage point; it has a bias. The
bias of the Bible is from the vantage point of the underclass.
But what happens if we lose sight of the prophetically

subversive vantage point of the Bible? What happens if those on top read themselves into the story, not as imperial Egyptians, Babylonians, and Romans, but as the Israelites? That's when you get the bizarre phenomenon of the elite and entitled using the Bible to endorse their dominance as God's will. This is Roman Christianity after Constantine. This is Christendom on crusade. This is colonizers seeing America as their promised land and the native inhabitants as Canaanites to be conquered. This is the whole history of European colonialism. This is Jim Crow. This is the American prosperity gospel. This is the domestication of Scripture. This is making the Bible dance a jig for our own amusement.

As Jesus preached the arrival of the kingdom of God he would frequently emphasize the revolutionary character of God's reign by saying things like, "The last will be first and the first last." How does Jesus' first-last aphorism strike you? I don't know about you, but it makes this modern day Roman a bit nervous.

Imagine this: A powerful charismatic figure arrives on the world scene and amasses a great following by announcing the arrival of a new arrangement of the world where those at the bottom are to be promoted and those on top are to have their lifestyle "restructured." How do people receive this? I can imagine the Bangladeshis saying, "When do we start?!" and the Americans saying, "Hold on now, let's not get carried away!"

Now think about Jesus announcing the arrival of God's kingdom with the proclamation of his counterintuitive Beatitudes. When Jesus said, "Blessed are the meek, for they shall inherit the earth," how was that received? Well, it depends on who is hearing it. The poor Galilean peasant would hear it as good news (gospel), while the Roman in his villa would hear it with deep suspicion. (I know it's an anachronism, but I can imagine Claudius saying something like, "Sounds like socialism to me!")

And that's the challenge I face in reading the Bible. I'm not the Galilean peasant. Who am I kidding! I'm the Roman in his villa and I need to be honest about it. I too can hear the gospel of the kingdom as good news (because it is!), but first I need to admit its radical nature and not try to tame it to endorse my inherited entitlement.

I am a (relatively) wealthy white American male, which is fine, but it means I have to work hard at reading the Bible right. I have to see myself basically as aligned with Pharaoh, Nebuchadnezzar, and Caesar. In that case, what does the Bible ask of me? Voluntary poverty? Not necessarily. But certainly the Bible calls me to deep humility — a humility demonstrated in hospitality and generosity. There's nothing necessarily wrong with being a relatively well-off white American male, but I better be humble, hospitable, and generous!

If I read the Bible with the appropriate perspective and humility I don't use the story of the Rich Man and Lazarus as a proof-text to condemn others to hell. I use it as a reminder that I'm a rich man and Lazarus lies at my door. I don't use the conquest narratives of Joshua to justify Manifest Destiny. Instead I see myself as a Rahab who needs to welcome newcomers. I don't fancy myself as Elijah calling down fire from heaven. I'm more like Nebuchadnezzar who needs to humble himself lest I go insane.

I have a problem with the Bible, but all is not lost. I just need to read it standing on my head. I need to change my perspective. If I can accept that the Bible is trying to lift up those who are unlike me, then perhaps I can read the Bible right.

CHAPTER 4

EXILE ON MAIN STREET

My favorite Rolling Stones album is their 1972 garage band masterpiece, *Exile On Main Street*. Recorded while the band was living as tax exiles in the south of France, Keith Richards gave the record its title in homage of their exile status. Exile on Main Street is also an apt turn of phrase for describing the Christian's somewhat ambiguous relationship with nationality. Christians are on Main Street as citizens in the nation of their citizenship, but they are never fully at home in it. We're on Main Street, but we're also exiles on Main Street. This is the tension created by baptism—from the moment we are baptized into the body of Christ we become expatriates in the land of our birth. This is how early Christians understood their relationship to nationality. The second-century *Epistle to Diognetus*, written by an anonymous Christian apologist for a pagan audience, explains how Christians simultaneously live as both citizens and exiles.

> Christians are no different from other people in terms of their country, language, or customs. Nowhere do they inhabit cities of their own, use a strange dialect, or live out of the ordinary…They inhabit both Greek and barbarian cities, according to the lot assigned to each. And they show forth the character of their own citizenship in a marvelous and admittedly paradoxical way by following local customs in what they wear and what they eat and in the rest of

their lives. They live in their respective countries but only as resident aliens; they participate in all things as citizens, and they endure all things as foreigners.[1]

Commenting on this passage Alan Kreider says,

> The nameless writer of this letter identifies the Christians with their neighbors. Christians are ordinary: they live in the same *insulae*, wear the same kind of clothing, speak with the same idioms and accents as other people, and eat the local foods. But Christians are also extraordinary. They know the tension between their two citizenships that expresses itself in a commitment to the local culture that is clear but conditional…As a result, the Christians are a hybrid people. They are *paroikoi*, resident aliens, living locally and participating in society, but not as full citizens.[2]

What the writer of the Epistle to Diognetus calls resident aliens and Alan Kreider calls hybrid people, I call exiles on Main Street. (It's only rock 'n' roll, but I like it.) But living as Christian exiles on Main Street can be a lot more demanding than living as rock star tax exiles in the south of France. For early Christians to live as exiles was risky and sometimes deadly. Being true to a Christian exile identity while living on Main Street in the Roman Empire is what populated the noble fellowship of the martyrs during the first three centuries of church history. Writing about the twelve famous North African Christian martyrs executed by the Roman government in Carthage in the year 180 (seven men and five women), Rowan Williams says,

> These Christians, most of them probably domestic slaves, had to explain to the magistrate that they were quite happy to pray for the imperial state and even to pay taxes, but that they could not grant the state their absolute allegiance. They had another loyalty—which did not mean that they wished to overthrow the administration, but that

they would not comply with the state's demands in certain respects. They would not worship the emperor, and, as we know from some other texts, refused to serve in the Roman army.[3]

The twelve North African Christians hauled before the Roman magistrate during the reign of Marcus Aurelius made it clear that they would render Caesar his due with respect and taxes, but in rendering to God what is God's alone they could not worship Caesar or participate in war. As a result of their fidelity to God they received the honor of becoming the first Christian martyrs in Africa. Fidelity to God in a world of idolatry sometimes calls for heroic faith. This kind of faith has an ancient pedigree. Long before Christians in the Roman Empire had to navigate the treacherous waters of living in an empire while reserving absolute allegiance for God alone, the monotheistic faith of Jews living as exiles in Babylon required them to do the same thing. After the first wave of Jewish captives was deported to Babylon in 597 BC, many of the newly arrived exiles cultivated a misplaced hope that their situation was only temporary. Prophets among the exiles confidently assured the people that they would soon return to their lives and homes in Jerusalem. But the irascible prophet Jeremiah was saying something entirely different. Jeremiah prophesied that Jerusalem was doomed to destruction and that soon the entire population of the city would be carried off as captives to Babylon. To counter the spurious hope propagated by false prophets, Jeremiah wrote a letter to the exiles in Babylon.

These are the words of the letter that the prophet Jeremiah sent from Jerusalem to the remaining elders among the exiles and to the priests, the prophets, and all the people, whom Nebuchadnezzar had taken into exile from Jerusalem to Babylon...Thus says the LORD of hosts, the God of Israel, to all the exiles whom I have sent into exile from Jerusalem to Babylon: Build houses and live in them; plant gardens and eat what they produce. Take

wives and have sons and daughters; take wives for your
sons, and give your daughters in marriage, that they may
bear sons and daughters; multiply there, and do not
decrease. But seek the welfare of the city where I have sent
you into exile, and pray to the LORD on its behalf, for in
its welfare you will find your welfare.[4]

In his letter Jeremiah was telling the exiles, "I know Babylon isn't
really your home, but you're going to have make it your home for now.
You're going to be in Babylon for a long time—at least seventy years—
so learn to make the best of it." And so they did. The Jewish exiles made
Babylon their home. They became exiles on Main Street in Babylon.
But after a couple of generations many of the Jews became *too* good at
being at home in Babylon. As Jeremiah's letter had exhorted them, they
built homes, got married, had sons and daughters, but as is often the
case with refugees, exiles, and immigrants, later generations don't always
see themselves as displaced, coming to regard the country of their exile
as their true home. That's what happened to the Jewish exiles living in
Babylon in the sixth century BC. They were in danger of becoming so at
home in Babylon that they would lose their identity as the chosen
people of Yahweh. To put it simply, these Jews were in danger of
becoming Babylonian. Assimilation now threatened to become apostasy.
This is what the prophetic books of Ezekiel and Daniel are about—how
to be the people of God while living as exiles in a pagan land.

The book of Daniel in particular, in wonderfully creative ways, is
designed to show Jews how to live in a pagan empire without becoming
pagan, but also, hopefully, without getting killed. Daniel is a tutorial on
how to survive but not apostatize. Most biblical scholars believe the
book of Daniel was written in the second century BC during the
Hellenization program of the Seleucid king Antiochus IV Ephiphanes
who persecuted Jews in an effort to force them to adopt Greek custom,
culture, and religion. Drawing upon memories and stories from their
experience in Babylon centuries earlier, the book of Daniel was
composed to teach Jews how to walk the narrow line of surviving in a
pagan empire without compromising their fidelity to the God of Israel.

By setting the book in Babylon during the sixth century instead of the Seleucid Empire of the second century, the anti-empire stories in Daniel were less dangerous during the persecution of Antiochus. But the lessons on faithful survival drawn from the Jewish experience in Babylon could easily be applied to contemporary Jews living under the rule of the Seleucid Empire. Daniel is about how to live responsibly but faithfully in an idolatrous culture. Thus Daniel is a book that's always relevant for the people of God—whether ancient Jews living in Babylon or early Christians living in Rome or modern Christians living in America.

In the vast narrative of Hebrew Scripture, one of the grand themes is that the people of Israel were to be Yahweh's alternative to pagan empire. When God chose a people who would embody fidelity and justice in a world of idolatry and injustice, God chose the seed of Abraham—an oppressed immigrant minority providing cheap labor for the Egyptian empire. Economic superpowers always need a source of cheap labor to support their affluent lifestyle—whether to bake their bricks or pick their cotton—and they generally prefer to exploit an ethnic minority that can be readily identified as an outcast "other." Oppressors have an easier time psychologically justifying their cruelty if their victims are a vilified other. For the Egyptian elite, the Hebrews were the ethnic minority other. But God sees it all. The book of Exodus tells how Yahweh heard the groans and saw the suffering of the Semitic slaves toiling in the brickyards and raised up a deliverer for them. Judgment Day now loomed on the Egyptian horizon. Pharaoh and the princes of Egypt were about to find out the hard way that Hebrew Lives Matter. Directed by the divine I AM encountered in the burning bush, Moses returned from the wilderness to issue Pharaoh the divine imperative, "Let my people go!" After a bit of persuasion from God (ten plagues!), Moses brought the Hebrews out of Egypt, through the Red Sea, and led them on their long trek to the promised land. This was the birth of a nation—a nation of former slaves who had surprisingly been adopted as God's own people. This kind of story should make the thoughtful Bible reader wonder where we find Jesus in the formative years of America—was Jesus guiding Thomas Jefferson and Andrew

Jackson in the White House, or was he picking cotton in Mississippi and walking the Trail of Tears?

The most distinctive thing about the nation of Israel in the ancient world was their requisite monotheism. To be the people of Yahweh meant to worship only one God. This was an unprecedented theology. The radical new idea of monotheistic worship was canonized in Israel's most sacred creed, the *Shema*: "Hear, O Israel: The LORD our God, the LORD is one. You shall love the LORD your God with all your heart and with all your soul and with all your might."[5] The most sacred aspect of Israel's Sinai covenant with Yahweh was the command that they would worship no other gods—they would worship Yahweh alone.

But being a monotheistic people in a polytheistic world put enormous pressure on Israel, and they faced the greatest challenge to their monotheism when the Temple of Yahweh and the city of Jerusalem were destroyed by the Babylonian king Nebuchadnezzar. After their forced deportation, the Hebrew people were once again slaves—this time in Babylon. As they hung their harps on willows and sat down by the rivers of Babylon and wept, the seed of Abraham faced a bitter test of their monotheistic covenant. Faithful Jews couldn't simply add new gods to their religion or switch their devotion to new Babylonian gods. In the ancient Gentile world, a conquered people were expected to worship the gods of their new overlords, but this was not an option for Jews; they couldn't blithely adopt the Babylon pantheon, begin to worship Bel and Nebo, and *still be* Jews. For Jews it was monotheism or bust. The survival of Jewish identity required faithfulness to Yahweh alone, despite the catastrophe that had befallen them. But how do you maintain fidelity to the living God when the pagans have prevailed? This is what the book of Daniel is about.

In Babylon, the Jewish exiles learned how to practice a creative and ongoing resistance while trying to stay alive in a pagan empire. The book of Daniel wrestles with the problem of being Jewish in a culture that doesn't want you to be Jewish. It's about living as a Jewish exile trying to survive on Babylon's Main Street. To hear the well-known stories of Daniel as children's Sunday School lessons is safe and easy—romantic tales about fiery furnaces and lions' dens from a time long ago in a world far away. What's *not* safe and what's *not* easy is to pull those stories into our present context and take the imaginative leap to *be* Daniel in the lion's den, to *be* Shadrach, Meshach, and Abednego in the fiery furnace, to *be* Jewish exiles on Babylon's Main Street. What's *not* easy or safe is to ask what it means to be a Christian in a culture that doesn't want you to actually live according to the Jesus way. In a culture that may wear a thin veneer of Christian civic religion but in truth venerates Mars and Mammon, what does it look like to maintain fidelity to the Prince of Peace who says you cannot serve God and money? These are highly relevant questions. Just as the book of Daniel spoke to second-century BC Jews living in the Seleucid Empire, so the book of Daniel speaks to twenty-first-century Christians living in the American Empire.

The book of Daniel opens with a story about four Jewish exiles living in Babylon—four promising youths selected for high-ranking civil service positions in the royal administration of King Nebuchadnezzar. Ashpenaz, the king's chief of staff, selected the most talented among the Hebrew exiles for a three-year training program. Among those selected were four prodigies from the tribe of Judah, all with good Jewish names: Daniel (God Is My Judge), Hananiah (Yahweh Is Gracious), Mishael (Who Is Like God?), and Azariah (Yahweh Has Helped). The first thing the chief of staff in charge of the recruits did was to give these Jews new Babylonian names. Daniel was to be called Belteshazzar (Bel's Prince), and Daniel's three friends were to be called Shadrach (Friend of the King), Meshach (Guest of the King), and Abednego (Servant of Nebo). It's obvious that Ashpenaz is intent on erasing their Jewish identity and transforming them into friends and servants of the Babylonian empire with its pantheon of patron gods. The self-identity derived from a name—what we call ourselves—forms us in significant ways. This is why early Christian converts from paganism would be given a "Christian name" at their baptism. For example, a woman named Invidia (the Roman goddess of retribution) might be given the new name of Christa at her baptism to signify that she had renounced the Roman gods and pledged her allegiance to Christ alone. Deep within our cultural habits and rituals are religious ideas designed to form us in significant ways. In the first chapter of Daniel, Ashpenaz wants the Jewish recruits to embrace the Babylonian gods, so as part of the indoctrination program Ashpenaz seeks to immerse (baptize) Daniel and his friends into Babylonian religion and culture. But Daniel and his friends are determined to only go so far—they will adapt where they can, but resist where they must.

Keeping a kosher diet was a crucial part of Daniel and his friends' covert resistance to paganism and to maintaining Jewish identity while immersed in a Babylonian culture. Unfortunately, there was a lot of pork on the royal menu for the civil servants in training. So Daniel made the risky move to ask permission for him and his friends to keep a simple kosher diet. Ashpenaz was initially hesitant but finally agreed to a ten-day test period. And, of course, at the end of the ten-day trial "Daniel and his three friends looked healthier and better nourished than the young men who had been eating the food assigned by the king."[6] This is the first story in the book of Daniel—a story of God's faithfulness to four Jewish youths who are committed to maintaining their Jewish identity by keeping a kosher diet while living in Babylon. Ultimately, the story isn't about giving up bacon and proving vegetables are healthier; the story is about holding onto a covenant identity in a pagan culture.

So how do we make the imaginative leap to apply Daniel's first story to our own lives? Despite what a few aberrant sects might claim, Christianity doesn't have dietary laws. As Christians we are free to put what we like in our stomachs, but Jesus warns us to guard what we let into our hearts. (See Mark 7:14–23) Just as Daniel and his friends living in the Babylonian empire had to be scrupulous about keeping kosher in an effort to maintain their Jewish identity, so Christians living in a modern empire must be scrupulous about what they feed on in an effort to maintain their baptismal identity. But what does that look like? What does it mean for a Christian to refuse to eat from the kitchen of empire? Well, what's the empire cooking? Mostly a steady diet of consumerism and militarism. It's the menu of Mammon and Mars. Obviously, an empire employing Christian civic religion as its cover doesn't use that language. Instead, a Christendom empire talks about economy and security—but you can tell by the reverent deference paid to "The Economy" and "Our National Security" that we have broached upon the sacred. As Jesus said, "Out of the abundance of the heart the mouth speaks."[7]

In the American experience, the economy is the most sacred obsession—all things are justified in the name of the economy. There's a reason why "It's the economy, stupid" has become an unassailable proverb in American politics. In the civic religion of Americanism, "It's the economy, stupid" always trumps "Love your neighbor as yourself." In a culture supremely committed to the economy, a president can sink to the lowest moral ebb as long as the Dow runs high. But if you feed on that lie, it will poison your heart and compromise your Christian identity. Prioritizing the economy above principle changes Christians into de facto pagans. The other sacred obsession in the American superpower is security. We guarantee our prosperity by a demonic devotion to the capacity to unleash hyper-violence upon our enemies. It's why the maintenance of a multi-trillion-dollar war machine appears perfectly reasonable rather than ludicrously insane. You can't claim to trust in God *and* spend trillions on weapons. Jesus put it bluntly when he said, "For where your treasure is, there your heart will be also."[8] And centuries before Christ, the psalmist said, "Some trust in chariots and some in horses, but we trust in the name of the LORD our God."[9] Gentiles may trust in their military budgets, but Israel was to trust in God. It's why the Torah commanded the kings of Israel not to multiply warhorses—a command they diligently ignored. The kings of Israel ignored Moses' command not to multiply warhorses just like every so-called Christian empire has ignored Christ's command to "put your sword away!"[10]

If you pay attention to what is said in the world political rhetoric, you will notice that the public liturgies of empire are all about the veneration of economy and security—consumerism and militarism. It's the royal diet. But you don't have to eat the empire's fare. Push your plate back like Daniel and keep Christian kosher. Refuse to feed on the lies of empire that prioritize economy and security above everything else—refuse the idolatrous devotion to Mammon and Mars. Christians should know better than to venerate economy and security as untouchable idols. Christians should know that the ineffable sacred is found in something other than the Dow and defense budgets. Christians should know that now abide faith, hope, and love. But if you feed on the empire's liturgies of economy and security, you will be formed in the opposite of faith, hope, and love—a malformation of the human soul that is perhaps best described as fear. This kind of fear is a spiritual pathology ensuing from a toxic diet. So refuse it. Feed instead on a kosher, anti-empire diet that nourishes faith, hope, and love. Feed on a lot more Philippians and a lot less Fox News. Feed on a lot more Luke and a lot less Rush. If like Daniel and his friends we refuse the fare of the empire's propaganda, it will be evident that we are far healthier than those feeding on the fear-inducing menu of Mammon and Mars. Those who feed on faith, hope, and love stand out in a culture characterized by fear; they are distinguished by the healthy glow of a robust peace. But it should be acknowledged that standing bravely in a culture that bows down to fear is not always safe...as Shadrach, Meshach, and Abednego found out.

King Nebuchadnezzar wielded supreme authority over the greatest military empire of his time—he was easily the most powerful man in the world. He was also a paranoid man. (The powerful are often inordinately paranoid; after all, when you're on top there's nowhere to go but down.) Babylon's economy and military was on top of the world, but the Commander-in-Chief was having nightmares. The book of Daniel says, "Nebuchadnezzar had such disturbing dreams that he couldn't sleep."[11] If we're paying close attention, we recognize we've already heard this story in the Bible. The Bible repeats itself because history repeats itself. Just as the fabulously wealthy Pharaoh had been haunted by dreams of scarcity in the days of Joseph, now the fabulously powerful Nebuchadnezzar is haunted by dreams of insecurity. Just as Pharaoh had to have a Jewish slave (Joseph) interpret his bad dream, now Nebuchadnezzar needs another Jewish slave (Daniel) to interpret his bad dream.

Nebuchadnezzar's troubling dream was about a giant statue made of gold, silver, bronze, iron, and clay that was eventually destroyed by "a stone cut without human hands" and blown away "like the chaff of the summer threshing floor."[12] The once imposing statue was replaced by "a great mountain that covered the whole earth." Nebuchadnezzar didn't know what it all meant, but he had an intuition that it was bad news for the king and his empire. When the king's astrologers and counselors, the Chaldean Intelligence Agency (CIA), proved incapable of deciphering the dream, Daniel rose to the occasion and explained to the king that the dream basically meant the Babylonian empire had an expiration date and that its demise would come sooner than later. The final interpretation of the dream was a prophecy that "the God of heaven will set up a kingdom that shall never be destroyed."[13] This reference to Yahweh's kingdom breaking into earth from heaven—a century and a half before the birth of Christ—is an Old Testament reference to what Jesus will later call the kingdom of God/heaven.

It's fascinating to notice that the dreams of the prophets and the nightmares of kings are often one and the same. For example, Isaiah sees a day when "the mountain of the LORD's house shall be established as the highest of the mountains"[14] and we call it a dream; when Nebuchadnezzar sees the same thing, he calls it a nightmare. Whether you interpret the kingdom of heaven as an optimistic dream or a haunting nightmare depends on what you're hoping for. Those looking for a heaven-sent revolution that rearranges the social order for human flourishing see it as a hopeful dream, but those deeply invested in maintaining a status quo of privilege for the elite see it as a dreadful nightmare. This much is certainly true: the in-breaking of heaven's government does indeed upset the status quo; as Jesus said regarding the advent of the kingdom of heaven, "Many who are first will be last, and the last will be first."[15] So think about it—if you're the most powerful man in the world, it's almost impossible not to hear this news as bad news or experience this dream as a nightmare. If our gospel is not heard as somewhat threatening to the one percent who are most privileged by the current arrangement of things, we may want to question if our evangelistic news is really gospel. If our gospel is not *especially* good news to the poor, Jesus and his apostles would not recognize it as the gospel of the kingdom they proclaimed. Sadly, the church after

Constantine has a long history of assuring their rich and powerful benefactors that the gospel is a spiritual message about how to go to a spiritual heaven after they die, and so they need not be concerned about the kingdom of heaven challenging their earthly privilege here and now.

Daniel, on the other hand, was not nearly as timid and dared to tell Nebuchadnezzar that Babylon's future was not secure because the sovereign Lord of heaven rules over the nations. Daniel was a true prophet. And despite the ominous interpretation of the dream (from the king's point of view), Daniel's ability to interpret the dream was rewarded with a promotion to a high-ranking position in Nebuchadnezzar's administration. Daniel's three friends Hananiah, Mishael, and Azariah (or as we have come to know them—Shadrach, Meshach, and Abednego) were awarded positions as provincial governors. But that's not the end of the story.

Sometime later, after the trauma of the king's nocturnal visions had abated, we are told that, "King Nebuchadnezzar made a golden statue whose height was sixty cubits and whose width was six cubits; he set it up on the plain of Dura in the province of Babylon."[16] This is Nebuchadnezzar's attempt to reject the divine dream/nightmare Daniel had interpreted. Instead of a deteriorating statue of gold, silver, bronze, iron, and clay destined to be destroyed and replaced by the mountain of God's own kingdom, the king of Babylon constructed a statue of gold— gold from head to toe. The symbolism is obvious: Babylon's golden age will endure forever. Empires love that kind of rhetoric, whether it's Rome as the "Eternal City" or America's *Novus Ordo Seclorum* (New Order of the Ages) on the Great Seal of the United States, found on the back of every dollar bill. In a bid to claim eternal glory, King Nebuchadnezzar erected on the plain of Dura a hundred-foot golden rejection of the kingdom of heaven. Think of it as the king of Babylon giving Yahweh a giant middle-finger salute—a gold finger.

The statue was a monument to Babylon's eternal glory, and it needed to be dedicated with sufficient ceremonial grandeur. Pomp and circumstance were required. A new anthem was composed to imbue the gold statue with a regal air. A command was given that when the Babylonian national anthem was played everyone was to make obeisance before the imperial image. To make sure everyone complied with Babylon's policy of enforced patriotism, a penalty for noncompliance was attached to the new law and the sanction was quite straightforward: "Anyone who refuses to obey will immediately be thrown into a blazing furnace."[17]

A grandiose dedication of the statue in Dura was arranged and all the provincial governors were to be in attendance. King Nebuchadnezzar himself would preside over the ceremony. A band would belt out "Hail to the Chief," patriotic speeches would be made, a fancy ribbon would be cut, and finally the anthem would sound and all would bow to the New Order of the Ages. And what about the three Jewish governors? Up to this point Shadrach, Meshach, and Abednego had been able to serve in their high-ranking public service positions without undue compromise of their Jewish identity. These exiles on Main Street had good jobs with generous benefits and great pension plans. But what now? To bow down to the gold icon of Babylonian greatness would be a violation of the first two commandments. It was either Yahweh's kingdom that was truly eternal or Nebuchadnezzar's kingdom, but it couldn't be both. Shadrach, Meshach, and Abednego had arrived at the crucible of dual citizenship...and it was a literal crucible! These three Jewish exiles were willing to faithfully serve the civil interests of Babylon as good governors, but when push came to shove, they stood their ground in fidelity to the God of Israel and would not bow to the imperial image. What happened next is one of the great stories of the Bible.

> Accordingly, at this time certain Chaldeans came forward and denounced the Jews. They said to King Nebuchadnezzar, "O king, live forever! You, O king, have made a decree, that everyone who hears the sound of the horn, pipe, lyre, trigon, harp, drum, and entire musical ensemble, shall fall down and worship the golden statue, and whoever does not fall down and worship shall be thrown into a furnace of blazing fire. There are certain Jews whom you have appointed over the affairs of the

province: Shadrach, Meshach, and Abednego. They pay no heed to you, O king. They do not serve your gods and they do not worship the golden statue that you have set up."[18]

That's when the king's head exploded. There's something about not paying public homage to the emblems of empire that evokes almost maniacal rage among kings and their courtiers. Shadrach, Meshach, and Abednego's Chaldean accusers summed up the charges quite neatly when they said, "They do not serve your gods." True enough. These Jewish exiles could serve the common good of Babylon, but they could not serve the patron gods of Babylon. Nebuchadnezzar interrogated the recalcitrant governors, and in an act of uncharacteristic patience was even willing to give the exiles a second chance by playing the national anthem one more time, but Shadrach and company told the king there was no need.

> Shadrach, Meshach, and Abednego answered the king, "O Nebuchadnezzar, we have no need to present a defense to you in this matter. If our God whom we serve is able to deliver us from the furnace of blazing fire and out of your hand, O king, let him deliver us. But if not, be it known to you, O king, that we will not serve your gods and we will not worship the golden statue you have set up."[19]

Now completely infuriated, the king didn't say Shadrach, Meshach, and Abednego—ethnic minorities with high-paying jobs—should be fired, he said they should be *thrown into the fire!* As the writer of Daniel tells it, "Nebuchadnezzar was so furious with Shadrach, Meshach, and Abednego that his face became distorted with rage as he commanded the furnace to be heated seven times hotter than usual."[20] There is an element of comedy in the telling of the story—try to imagine Nebuchadnezzar's face contorted into a ludicrous mask of fury while sputtering, "Seven times hotter!" What a bigheaded and pompous buffoon! But the king is the king, so the furnace of patriotic rage was stoked sevenfold, and the three Jewish exiles were tossed in. But as every Sunday School girl and boy knows, Nebuchadnezzar's visage of rage quickly gave way to a countenance of shocked astonishment. The beloved story of the Hebrew children in the fiery furnace finds its "happily ever after" ending when Nebuchadnezzar sees not three, but *four* men unharmed in the midst of the flames, and as the astonished king said, "The fourth is like the Son of God."[21] Shadrach, Meshach, and Abednego defied the king and lived to tell about it. Allow me to tell the story with an anachronism that makes the point. In the face of the Third Reich, Shadrach, Meshach, and Abednego signed the Barmen Declaration and were then delivered from the megalomaniac intentions of the Führer. That's the happy ending version of the story that we find in Daniel. But we know that fidelity to God doesn't always result in a reprieve from suffering and martyrdom, as Dietrich Bonheoffer and Martin Niemöller can testify...and as millions of twentieth-century Jews can testify. Yet I find consolation in my conviction that the fourth man "like the Son of God" was in the furnace with each and every one of them.

The book of Daniel, most likely written in the second century BC, was intended to help Jews figure out how to survive the forced Hellenization program of the Seleucid Empire while maintaining fidelity to the God of Israel. Two and half centuries later, the book of Revelation was written to warn Christians living in the Roman Empire about the seductive nature of the Great Harlot of Rome, cryptically called Babylon. Toward the end of the book of Revelation, a voice from heaven calls out to Christians living in the empire saying, "Come out of her, my people, so that you do not take part in her sins, and so that you do not share in her plagues."[22] Jews living in Babylon were literal exiles—a diaspora living in a foreign land. Christians living in the metaphorical Babylon of Rome were metaphorical exiles—they were indigenous to the empire, but had been made exiles by their baptism. Today, American Christians are metaphorical exiles within the modern empire of America. But most do not see themselves as exiles. Most fail to see American culture as something we need to come out of. Instead of coming out of an American culture built on consumerism and militarism and being the church, many Christians are attempting to return to a mythical past where they imagine America as a kind of New Israel. All of this is tragically mistaken. Until we see America as a kind of New Babylon instead of a kind of New Israel, it will be exceedingly difficult, if not impossible, for Christians to faithfully embody the holy otherness of the kingdom of Christ. If America is the "New Order of the Ages," then what is the kingdom of Christ? This needs to be made clear: America is not an extension of the kingdom of Christ, America is a continuation of Babylon. America may (or may not be) a gentler, kinder Babylon, but it's a Babylon nonetheless. To put it another way, King Jesus is not the best version of Caesar; King Jesus is the anti-Caesar. This is what "Jesus is Lord" has always meant.

CHAPTER 5

IN THE TIME OF TYRANT KINGS

I f you visit the biblical sites in Israel and Palestine, you will encounter the inescapable presence of King Herod the Great (*circa* 74–4 BC). Herod, the first and greatest king of the Herodian dynasty, was an indefatigable builder obsessed with grandiose edifices that have left an indelible mark upon the geography that was the backdrop for the life of Jesus. Among King Herod's greatest architectural accomplishments are the Temple in Jerusalem, the harbor at Caesarea Maritima, the mountaintop fortress of Masada, and a man-made mountain (the highest peak in the Judean desert!) three miles southeast of Bethlehem that is the site of Herodium, Herod's most imposing palace and almost certainly the location of his tomb. Along with Caesar Augustus, Mark Antony, and Cleopatra—with whom he was variously associated—Herod the Great is one of the towering figures in the drama of the Roman world of the first century BC. There is no denying that Herod the Great was indeed great according to a non-Christian idea of greatness. He was great in ability, great in ambition, and especially great in his ruthless authoritarianism. Herod was both illustrious and iniquitous. Along with his military prowess and architectural acumen, King Herod was also a paranoid tyrant who maintained a secret police and was notorious for executing his political rivals—including one of his wives (he married nine times) and two of his sons. But his infamous act—the act that insured Herod would be a household name forever—was his attempted assassination of a political rival when the rival was only a baby. Welcome to the dark side of Christmas.

Matthew's Epiphany chapter begins with these words: "In the time of King Herod..."[1] As the Gospel of Matthew tells us, Jesus was born in the time of King Herod, and the history books tell us that most of civilization has been lived in the time of kings like Herod—that is, in the time of tyrant kings. I'm talking about the time of Herod, the time of Pharaoh, the time of Nebuchadnezzar, the time of Augustus, the time of Nero, all the way into modern times—the time of Hitler and Mussolini, the time of Franco and Salazar, the time of Pinochet and Putin. It's tragically true that most people have lived their lives in the time of tyrant kings. But the gospel also announces the glad tidings that with the birth of Jesus heaven has invaded the time of tyrant kings!

Matthew tells the story of the first gentiles to receive the revelation (epiphany) of Christ the King. This is the beloved Christmas story of the Wise Men. These Oriental magi (or magicians) were most likely Zoroastrian priests from Persia skilled in astronomy, astrology, and dream interpretation who evidently somehow discerned in the stars an astrological sign announcing the birth of a new King of the Jews. The Zoroastrian priests regarded this birth as so auspicious that they embarked upon a dangerous and difficult thousand-mile journey from Persia to Judea in order to perform obeisance before the child and present their famous gifts of gold, frankincense, and myrrh. Because the magi were looking for a child king born in Judea, it made sense for them to inquire in the capital city of Jerusalem, but by doing so they unwittingly set in motion terrible events.

When Jesus was born, King Herod was nearing seventy and had reigned over Judea for more than thirty years. Herod was rich and powerful but increasingly paranoid. His paranoia may have stemmed from an anxious awareness of how tenuous his kingly position really was. Herod was the king of Judea but only as a vassal for the Roman Empire. Herod had been born to an Edomite father and a Jewish mother and did not descend from either the Davidic or Hasmonean royal line. In 37 BC, around the age of forty, Herod was granted the kingship of Judea by the Roman Senate as a reward for his loyalty to Rome during the Parthian War. Following the installation ceremony in Rome, Herod walked out of the Senate building arm in arm with the two most powerful men in the world—Caesar Augustus and Mark Antony. Herod then led a procession up Capitoline Hill to the Temple of Jupiter where the newly minted King of the Jews offered a sacrifice to the chief deity in the Roman imperial religion.[2] This should give you some idea why pious Jews were not thrilled with Herod as their king! It should also give you some idea of the kind of compromises a Jewish king would be required to make to stay in Rome's good graces.

Throughout his reign, Herod had to navigate the treacherous politics of simultaneously quelling popular Jewish uprisings while maintaining the favor of his Roman overlords. As a client king unpopular with the local Jewish population but pragmatically useful to Rome, Herod was always just one political revolt away from being sacked by Caesar Augustus. It seems that the strain of constant political intrigue had made Herod a pathologically paranoid king. So when a retinue of distinguished magi from Persia arrived in Jerusalem with the portentous news that a child had been born king of the Jews (not *made* king, but *born* king), Herod was more anxious than ever. The intelligence report from the magi informed Herod that the long-dead royal line of David had somehow revived and a legitimate successor to the throne of David had been born. Matthew tells the story of a child born in the time of tyrant kings owing tyrant kings nothing. This is the glad tidings of good politics brought to us at Christmas.

How did Herod take the surprising news of a revival in the lineage of King David? Not well. Herod had too much respect for the venerable magi to dismiss it as "fake news," so, as Matthew tells us, "When King Herod heard this, he was frightened, and all Jerusalem with him."[3] The birth announcement brought by the magi filled Herod with dread, and Herod's fear of a baby shows just how fragile his ego was. And Jerusalem was afraid too. The citizens of Jerusalem were well aware of how dangerous life can be when a powerful ruler with a fragile ego is afraid. So all of Jerusalem was on edge—anxious about what the paranoid king might do. What Herod did was commit one of the greatest crimes in the Bible—we call it the Slaughter of the Innocents. Though it's true we have no corroboration of this atrocity outside of Matthew's Gospel, the account is in keeping with what we know about Herod's ruthless methods. Matthew tells us that the paranoid king sent death squads to Bethlehem—a tiny village just three miles from the Herodium palace—with the ghastly instructions to kill all male babies under the age of two. The terrible massacre is commensurate with the predictable reaction of frightened kings and kingdoms who always deal in death—whether it's death squads by night or Predator drones by day. In his terror Herod had targeted one baby for assassination, but many babies would end up dying. The church has called this horror the Slaughter of the Innocents, but modern day kings and kingdoms have sanitized it with the Orwellian term "collateral damage."

I understand that most Christians don't like to sully their sentimental version of Christmas with Matthew's account of King Herod's collateral damage; it too easily reminds us of drone strikes in Afghanistan gone awry that end up hitting wedding parties instead of terrorist cells. But this is the unflinching report given to us by the Evangelist. So we let the dark side of Christmas speak to us. When contemporary superpowers adopt the ways of ancient tyrant kings, no matter how pragmatic the motives, we need to be honest about the fact that innocent people, even children, will be killed. We should always remember that the ends never justify the means; rather, the means are the ends in the process of becoming. If the means are death-dealing, the ends aren't going to be life-affirming. You can bomb the world to pieces, but you can't bomb the world to peace.

In her important book *How Everything Became War and the Military Became Everything*, Georgetown law professor and former Pentagon advisor Rosa Brooks describes the simultaneous banality and horror of modern drone warfare.

> They watch boys herding goats, and women carrying goods from the market. They see parents playing with their children, and armed men conferring in dusty compounds. Mostly, the clean-cut men and women at Creech [Air Force Base in Nevada] just observe, taking eight-hour shifts as they watch the endlessly unfolding images of lives lived far away. Occasionally, though, they

act—and with a few computer commands and a puff of smoke viewed on a video monitor, lives end in a burst of noise and searing heat.[4]

Killing from a keyboard. PlayStation soldiers. X-Box warriors. We may want to pretend that computerized drone warfare is a precise operation, but far too often innocent people, including children, are the slaughtered victims of the innocuous-sounding atrocity called collateral damage. The dark side of Christmas forces us to ask uncomfortable questions about babies who are killed by covert operations in the name of "security." In response to the inevitable and sometimes angry pushback of drawing political implications from the Christmas story, Stanley Hauerwas in his theological commentary on Matthew says,

> Too often the political significance of Jesus's birth, a significance that Herod understood all too well, is lost because the church, particularly the church in America, reads the birth as confirmation of the assumed position that religion has within the larger framework of politics. That is, the birth of Jesus is not seen as a threat to thrones and empires because religion concerns the private. Such a view does not intentionally downplay the importance of the gospel, since it is assumed that the private deals with the most important aspect of our life, which is often labeled "morality." The gospel of Matthew, however, knows no distinction between the public (the political) and the private. Jesus is born into time, threatening the time of Herod and Rome.[5]

Offering a prophetic perspective on King Herod's Slaughter of the Innocents, Matthew gives us a Christmas text that will never be found on any Christmas card:

"Then was fulfilled what had been spoken through the prophet Jeremiah:

'A voice was heard in Ramah,
    wailing and loud lamentation,
Rachel weeping for her children;
    she refused to be consoled, because they are no more.'"[6]

Rachel, the wife of Jacob, is one of the matriarchs of Judaism. Rachel died in childbirth and was buried just outside of Bethlehem. To this day whenever I cross the walled border separating Jerusalem and Bethlehem I pass the still venerated Tomb of Rachel. The prophet Jeremiah, living six centuries before Christ, saw Rachel as a kind of patroness of Hebrew children. Anticipating the brutal slaughter that would befall even children with the invasion of Nebuchadnezzar's armies, Jeremiah depicts Rachel weeping inconsolably over the slaughtered innocent children.[7] Six centuries later the Evangelist Matthew saw a further fulfillment of Jeremiah's dark prophecy, a terrible fulfillment that came to pass when Herod executed the baby boys of Bethlehem who had the cruel misfortune of being born a little too close to the birth of King Jesus.

Of course we know the story, and we know the baby king escaped the gruesome infanticide ordered by the paranoid king. An angel warned Joseph in a dream to take the baby and his mother and escape to Egypt. In the flight to Egypt we see the Holy Family as refugees, and once we have seen the Holy Family as refugees fleeing a violent Middle East despot, it must forever influence how Christians view modern-day refugees in similar situations—in the eyes of God, they too are a kind of holy family. These acts of prophetic imagination (to borrow a phrase from Walter Brueggemann) are necessary for those who would read the biblical Christmas story with contemporary relevance and not just romanticized sentimentality. One of the remarkable things about the Bible is that it doesn't paper over atrocity or shy away from giving vivid depictions of the brutality of life in the time of tyrant kings. We need to read the Bible as honestly as it is written and not try to domesticate it into the saccharine clichés of sentimental Christmas cards. For the light of the gospel to shine truthfully, we need to be honest about the darkness in which it shines.

Are we shocked by Herod's crime? Of course. But though we are horrified, we should not be surprised. Tyrant kings and kingdoms have a long history of ruthlessly dealing with threat and dissent, and this is exactly what we find described in Matthew's account of the Slaughter of the Innocents. Stanley Hauerwas says, "Rome knew how to deal with enemies; you kill them or co-opt them."[8] Usually the rich get co-opted and the poor get killed. The Temple elite of Jerusalem are bought off while the peasant babies of Bethlehem are killed. This is the darkness in which the light of the gospel comes to shine—"and the light shines in the darkness and the darkness did not overcome it."[9] Or as the Christmas carol about the little town of Bethlehem says, "Yet in thy dark streets shineth the everlasting light."

Jesus' invasion by birth into the dark time of tyrant kings gives us a choice: we can trust in the armed brutality of violent power or we can trust in the naked vulnerability of love. It seems like an absurd choice, but only one of these ways is the Jesus way. We have to choose between the old way of Caesar and the new way of Christ. It's the choice between the sword and the cross. We have to decide if we'll pledge our allegiance to the Empire of Power or the Empire of Love, but we can't do both. Following the Jesus way of loving enemies and doing good to those who hate us isn't necessarily safe and it doesn't mean we won't ever get hurt, but it does mean the darkness won't prevail.

If we make security our most cherished value (euphemistically referred to in America as "freedom"), we conspire with the principalities and powers to keep the world a dark place. But when in solidarity with Jesus we are willing to risk our safety for the sake of Christlike love, we are the light of the world, a city that cannot be hid. This is the great legacy of the Christian martyrs. Rome could take their lives, but Rome could not extinguish their light. In their deaths the Christian martyrs became iridescent lamps flooding the pagan darkness of the Roman Empire with the light of heaven. Roman emperors and governors could execute Christian men and women like Polycarp, Justin Martyr, Perpetua, Felicity, Saint Sebastian, Agnes, Cyprian, and countless others, but in their deaths their once obscure lives became enduring beacons of Christian faith, hope, and love.

When Jesus enjoins us to take up our cross and follow him, he is inviting us to join him in the risk of love. But what about those who want a risk-free Christianity of guaranteed security? If we are unwilling that we or our children should ever have to suffer for the name of Jesus, we concoct a Christianity where martyrdom is out of the question. And when martyrdom is no longer considered a possibility, we turn Christianity into a safe and anodyne civil religion in service of the empire. This is not the risky and robust Christianity of Peter and Paul, of Perpetua and Felicity, of Dietrich Bonhoeffer and Óscar Romero. For the Christian, martyrdom is always on the table—we signed up for the possibility of martyrdom with our baptism. In fact, in our baptism we have already died with Christ. But because the one who was crucified forgiving his enemies is the King of Glory raised from the dead, Christians believe that no matter what darkness and hate may do, in the end light and love will win. This is the kind of faith commended in one of Revelation's most beautiful anthems.

> "Then I heard a loud voice in heaven, proclaiming,
> 'Now have come the salvation and power
> and the kingdom of our God
> and the authority of our Messiah,
> for the accuser of our comrades has been thrown down,
> who accuses them day and night before our God.
> But they have conquered him by the blood of the Lamb
> and by the word of their testimony,
> for they did not cling to life even in the face of death.'"[10]

Tyrant kings and kingdoms are accustomed to controlling people through fear, especially through the threat of violence. But what do tyrant kings and kingdoms do with a people who see the world in a radically new way? A people who don't believe that the meaning of history is defined by war and violence? And, yes, such people exist...they were first called Christians at Antioch.[11] Eventually the new faith of these strange people spread throughout the entire Roman Empire. Noted sociologist of religion Rodney Stark estimates that by the early fourth century (prior to Constantine) the Christian population had grown to five or six million—or between eight and twelve percent of the Roman Empire.[12] It wasn't safe to be a Christian, but about one in ten persons living in the Roman Empire chose to become Christians anyway—despite threats and persecutions from emperors like Caligula, Nero, and Diocletian. The limitation of tyrant kings is that they can only control those who are afraid. The principalities and powers are adept at harnessing the fear of death—the fear of loss in all its forms—to control those who make their place of privilege possible. But those who have disarmed fear by being formed in maturing love ("perfect love casts out fear"[13]) are beyond the control of tyrant kings—even tyrant kings who would kill babies.

Those who through faith and baptism have replaced the crippling motive of fear with the liberating motive of love are a consistent challenge to those who would kill babies, whether for their convenience or for their cause. Those who follow Jesus are a prophetic challenge to abortion for convenience and a prophetic challenge to carpet-bombing for a cause. If it threatens the wellbeing of children, followers of Jesus oppose it. Nothing less is truly pro-life. This is why a consistent pro-life Christian ethic opposes the death-friendly practices of abortion, capital punishment, torture, war, predatory capitalism, environmental exploitation, unchecked proliferation of guns, neglecting the poor, refusing the refugee, and keeping healthcare unaffordable for millions. Using an anti-abortion position to provide moral cover for pro-death practices and policies advantageous to the principalities and powers should not be confused with a pro-life ethic derived from the life and teaching of Jesus Christ. As early as the second-century *Didache*, Christians have said abortion is incompatible with Christian ethics. But those same second-century Christians also said war is incompatible with Christian ethics. If we rightly claim that abortion for convenience is incompatible with Christian ethics because Christ was once in the womb, we must also recognize that refusing refugees is incompatible with Christian ethics because Christ was once forced to seek asylum in a foreign land. Christians must have their ethics informed by Christ, not by the vested interests of tyrant kings.

Much of the prophetic literature in the Hebrew Bible is a sustained critique of tyrant kings and kingdoms—Egypt, Assyria, Babylon, Persia, Greece. And by the time we arrive at the opening pages of the New Testament, it's Caesar Augustus and client kings like Herod who sit atop the pyramid structure of society, making sure tyranny benefits those on top. But now a new king is born—a king whose birth portends such significance that it draws magi from a thousand miles away and provokes a paranoid king to infanticidal rage. An alternative kingdom, a redemptive regime, has invaded earth. Joy to the world! Herod's days are numbered. The old king has one foot in the grave and his dynasty is headed for an ignoble end, while the new king whose kingdom will never end is wrapped in swaddling clothes, lying in a manger. The magi discerned the birth of the King of the Jews in the stars, but the king himself was born in a cave. It had to be that way. For in the kingdom of God, greatness is not achieved by reaching for the stars, but by love's willing descent into lowliness, meekness, and humility. The new King, the King of Kings, will not sit atop an elaborate pyramid scheme, but will stoop to wash the feet of his disciples. Something truly new entered the world at Bethlehem!

What does the kingdom of God look like? It looks like Jesus. It looks like the sick being healed, the poor being fed, the demonized being delivered, and the dead being raised. It looks like outsiders given a seat at the table and hypocritical gatekeepers given their comeuppance. It looks like forgiveness for sinners and a feast for all. If you can embrace the newness, it looks like a party where water turns to wine. If you resist the newness, it looks like judgment day when the whip comes down and tables are flipped. As the great theologian Origen of Alexandria (184–254) said, "Jesus is the kingdom in person."[14] So if it doesn't look like Jesus, it's not the kingdom of God. And if it's not the kingdom of God, we must never pledge our ultimate allegiance to it.

It's true that most of history has been lived in the time of tyrant kings, but the gospel is also true. And the birth of Christ opened a portal to an alternative time—the prophetic time imagined by the Hebrew poets and prophets. With the coming of Messiah our lives no longer have to be defined by the time of tyrant kings; we can embrace the time of the coming kingdom. We do it by faith. We do it by allowing the church to live up to its high calling to embody the reign of Christ here and now. We do it by taking our baptism seriously, confessing that the baptized belong to the age to come. This is the gospel of the kingdom proclaimed by Jesus and the Apostles.[15] This is not the privatized, minimized, postmortem gospel of how to go to heaven when you die while keeping the world as it has always been. No! This is the robust gospel that shames the principalities and powers and liberates the world and all its creatures for full flourishing!

The Epiphany account of Matthew ends with the death of King Herod—because even tyrant kings are subject to death. But when the baby born in Bethlehem came of age and began to preach around the age of thirty, there was another King Herod on the throne (Herod's son), because there's always another tyrant king to curate the old age. So we could say that it was still the time of Herod, the time of tyrant kings. But that's *not* what Jesus said! Instead, from the moment that he first began to preach in Galilee, Jesus announced the arrival of the kingdom from heaven.

> After John was arrested [by King Herod], Jesus went to Galilee preaching the Message of God: "Time's up! God's kingdom is here. Change your life and believe the Message."[16]

Jesus began announcing the arrival of the kingdom of God just after John the Baptist was arrested by King Herod. We almost get the feeling that the arrest of John prompted Jesus to take up where John had left off. John had been preaching, "Repent, for the kingdom of heaven has come near,"[17] and now Jesus began saying, "The kingdom of God has come near; repent, and believe in the good news."[18] With John in jail, the baton was passed, and now it's Jesus who is announcing the onset of God's kingdom. An important transition in the gospel story occurs when one of the most important figures is hauled off to jail. We should notice how remarkable it is that so many of the central characters in the story of the New Testament are arrested. John the Baptist, Jesus, all of the twelve disciples, Paul and his companions, John of Patmos—they all end up in jail at some point. We even have a genre of the New Testament known as "the prison epistles." This should alert us to the truth that the gospel is uncomfortably political. The gospel of the kingdom is not *partisan*—it will not serve the partisan interests of a particular political party—but it is intensely *political*. It's political because it poses a direct challenge to the principalities and powers and the way the world is arranged. What Herod and the rest of the ruling elite got right about the message of John the Baptist and Jesus of Nazareth was that it carried enormous political implications—political implications that motivated them to attack the kingdom of heaven. This is exactly what Jesus said after John was executed in prison.

> And from the time John the Baptist began preaching until now, the Kingdom of Heaven has suffered from violence, and violent people are attacking it.[19]

Tyrant kings did not violently attack the kingdom of heaven that John and Jesus were announcing because it was a purely spiritual kingdom affecting only the interior life or postmortem fate of the individual, but precisely because their gospel carried subversive political implications. John and Jesus were explicitly declaring that the kingdom of God was arriving, and implicitly declaring that the time of tyrant kings had expired. John was the forerunner preparing Israel for her true king. Jesus was that king—the Spirit-anointed Messianic king appointed to reign over a new kingdom established by God. But for Jesus to launch the kingdom of God, he needed to be crowned King of the Jews in the capital city of Jerusalem. An American president isn't inaugurated in Omaha, and the King of the Jews isn't crowned in Galilee. Jesus must go to Jerusalem. But this is dangerous. Jerusalem isn't the domain of the provincial peasantry eager for a change, Jerusalem is the stronghold of the principalities and powers benefitting from Roman rule—King Herod, Pontius Pilate, and Caiaphas the high priest. For a Galilean claiming kingship to march into Jerusalem is to guarantee a showdown. So between a year (according to the synoptic Gospels) and three years (according to the Gospel of John) after he began his ministry, Jesus and his followers leave Galilee and head for Jerusalem. They know an inevitable confrontation with the principalities and powers awaits them. Mark captures the dramatic tension of this march on Jerusalem when he says,

> They were on the road, going up to Jerusalem, and Jesus was walking ahead of them; they were amazed, and those who followed were afraid.[20]

Of course they were afraid; revolutionaries don't march into the teeth of the capital city without some trepidation. And though Jesus told his disciples exactly what would happen, they couldn't quite understand it.

> "See, we are going up to Jerusalem, and the Son of Man will be handed over to the chief priests and the scribes, and they will condemn him to death; then they will hand him over to the Gentiles; they will mock him, and spit upon him, and flog him, and kill him; and after three days he will rise again."[21]

The disciples could never quite understand what Jesus meant by being raised on the third day. They probably heard it as an idiom meaning that Jesus would be part of the resurrection of the righteous at the end of the age—some indefinable point in the unknown future, as when Hosea says, "After two days he will revive us, on the third day he will raise us up."[22] But when is the third day? And what the disciples could certainly not comprehend is how Jesus could become king and establish God's new kingdom if he were killed. A victorious Messiah has to kill his enemies, not be killed by them. Nevertheless, they marched on with Jesus, uncertain of what awaited them in Jerusalem. When some of the Pharisees warned Jesus to get out of Judea because Herod was seeking to kill him, Jesus said, "Go tell that fox, 'I will keep on driving out demons and healing people today and tomorrow, and on the third day I will reach my goal.'"[23] Despite foreboding and death threats, Jesus set his face to go to Jerusalem—and one way or another, something *big* was going to happen when Jesus arrived.

West of Shinar

God said, "Let there be."
Existence. Life. Awareness.
Good, very good
A man called Mankind
A woman called Life
They bore and wore the Imago Dei
Walked in the Garden with God

Then something went wrong
Paradise Lost
Moved to an apartment east of Eden
And had babies
Called them Cain and Abel
Farmer and Shepherd.
But the landed gentry murdered the nomadic herdsman
The killer lied to God (and himself) about what he
        had done
"I didn't murder my brother—I just killed an enemy.
        It had to be done."

Oh, Cain
A marked man
An exiled wanderer
Built the first city
Founded civilization
Established the pattern
Every king and kingdom followed suit
Pharaoh and Caesar
Egypt and Rome.
Call it all Babylon
They had bricks for stone, slime for mortar

(Masonry and weaponry. More like Mordor.)
The children of Cain, the sons of Nimrod—
They built
Pyramids and Parthenons
But always the bodies were hid.
So it was. So it was. So it was.

But those Jews…that seed of Abraham—
They had their poet-prophets
Who spoke of a Prince of Peace
Of swords and plowshares
Lions and lambs
Of course they were just poems. Weren't they?

Centuries roll by
A birth in Bethlehem
King of the Jews
Magi seek out
Herod freaks out
Babies are killed
Rachel weeps

Years roll by
First the Forerunner, then the Main Attraction
Good news!
The government of God is at hand!
Not so quick
The empire strikes back!
Condemned, crucified, killed
Dead and buried
Behind Caesar's seal
But God overrules!
Raised on the third day!
What does it all mean?
This!

For the first time in forever it's not a lion, a leopard, a
    bear, or a wolf—
But a Lamb who sits on the throne!
Worthy is the Lamb!

Redeemed civilization (New Jerusalem) is the City of
    the Lamb
No banners or anthems or monuments or memorials—
To hide the bodies of the slain
For it was the Lamb who was slain...but lives again
The dragon-accuser still says, "They're not your brothers."
(The ancient lie that crouched at Cain's door so long ago)
But the dragon-accuser is overcome—
By the blood of the Lamb and the word of testament
For the faithful would rather die than return to the
    way of Cain
Worthy is the Lamb!

Meanwhile outside the City the fires of war keep burning
Call it what it is, call it Gehenna, call it Hades, call it hell
But to those suffering from the suicide of a self-
    inflicted flame—
The Spirit and the Bride say, "Come!"
"Change your clothes, change your mind, and come
    on in!"
The Spirit and the Bride and the Lamb all beckon
    ...and wait
For her gates will never be shut

CHAPTER 6

THERE'S ALWAYS SOME DUDE ON A HORSE

In recent years Peri and I have fallen in love with Portugal. We were introduced to this enchanting country by my Portuguese publisher and now it's near the top of our daydream places to live a fantasy expat life. Exquisite seafood, Port wine, blue-tiled buildings, Baroque architecture, *Pastéis de Nata, Fado, Saudades,* José Saramago and António Lobo Antunes, the insane love of soccer, and the friends we've made there have all made Portugal a magical place for us. There's something romantic and appealing about has-been empires that have relinquished their lust to rule the world and are now content to simply enjoy life. Faded glory and noble decay can be a nice segue to good living. (The song "I Love Portugal" by the American recording artist Sun Kil Moon perfectly captures how I feel about the land of Lusitania.)

During our second trip to Portugal, we were strolling around Lisbon when we walked past the statue of some Portuguese general. This (unknown to me) military hero from long ago was astride a horse, with reins in one hand and a sword in the other. The statue embodied the imperial aspirations of a Portugal that is now long gone. In my travels I've seen this same statue in every capital city—the horse, the dude, the sword, the pigeon droppings. Of course, they're not really the same statue, but if you're a foreigner and don't know who the hero is, they all look the same. So I remarked to Peri, "There's always some dude on a horse." We laughed and it's become a running joke. Now we have to say it every time we see one of these statues. After working this quip into some of my sermons, people now regularly send me photos of these statues from around the world tagged with, "There's always some dude on a horse." I've seen horse-riding dudes in capitals from Lisbon to London, from Rome to Paris, from St. Petersburg to Washington D.C. Of course, the dude with a tricorn hat on a horse in D.C. is George Washington. It makes a difference if the dude is *your* dude. Most Americans upon beholding *this* marble dude will feel the kind of patriotic stirring in their bosom that the citizens of other lands feel for their equestrian statuary.

The statues are meant to memorialize military might and imperial conquest—that's why the riders always hold reins in one hand and a sword in the other. This also helps explain why horses are generally held in low regard in Scripture. It's not that God has anything against the beautiful animal that is the horse but because of its association with war. In the Bible, horses are almost always *war* horses. Mules and donkeys were beasts of burden and draft animals; horses were weapons of war. As Proverbs says, "The horse is made ready for the day of battle."[1] Thus the Song of Moses commemorates God's victory over the Egyptian army at the Red Sea by saying,

> I will sing to the LORD, for he has triumphed gloriously;
> horse and rider he has thrown into the sea.[2]

After they were given improbable victories over the Canaanites, Yahweh commanded Israel to "hamstring their [the Canaanites'] horses, and burn their chariots with fire."[3] The command to hamstring horses should not be read as an act of animal cruelty but rather as a prohibition of accumulating the means to wage large-scale wars of aggression. Once God had miraculously given Israel victory over the more powerful Canaanite nations, the Israelites were not to adopt militaristic ways or acquire the implements of war; instead they were to destroy the capacity to wage war. Israel was to be set on a trajectory of peaceable neighborliness, not warring aggression. We see this in the Torah where the kings of Israel are prohibited from stabling large numbers of horses[4]—a command that King Solomon clearly excelled at violating: "Solomon had four thousand stalls for horses and chariots and twelve thousand horses, which he stationed in the chariot cities."[5] It's this kind of reliance on equine militarism that the psalmist challenges when he writes,

> Some trust in chariots and some in horses,
>   but we trust in the name of the LORD our God.[6]

Most of us are easily impressed by glorious generals on their magnificent warhorses (or their modern equivalents), but Yahweh and his prophets are not. For example, the prophet Isaiah sees Jerusalem's trust in chariots and horses as idolatrous and a forsaking of the ways of Yahweh. After announcing that the reign of Messiah will be characterized by a renunciation of militarism where swords are turned into plowshares, spears into pruning hooks, war renounced, and military training abandoned,[7] Isaiah goes on to immediately denounce Israel's idolatrous militarism by saying,

> Come, descendents of Jacob,
> let us walk in the light of the LORD!
> For the LORD has rejected his people,
> the descendents of Jacob,
> because they have filled their land with practices from the East
> and with sorcerers, as the Philistines do.
> Israel is full of silver and gold;
> there is no end to its treasures.
> Their land is full of warhorses;
> there is no end to its chariots.
> Their land is full of idols;
> the people worship things they have made
> with their own hands.[8]

It might be pushing things too far to describe the ubiquitous statues of generals astride warhorses as idols, but these monuments clearly do represent a nationalistic infatuation with the ways and means of war—a ways and means countermanded by the peaceable reign of Messiah.

Without question the greatest of all the warhorse-riding world conquerors from antiquity was Alexander the Great (356–323 BC). We even know the name of his horse—probably the most famous animal in history: Bucephalus (355–326 BC). In less than a dozen years Alexander conquered the world from Greece to India before dying in Babylon at the age of thirty-two. Alexander was the epitome of greatness. He was tutored by the famous philosopher Aristotle and was a world emperor by the time he was thirty, dying in Babylon in the palace of none other than Nebuchadnezzar. Among those taught to revere heroic achievement and violent conquest, everything about Alexander's life evokes a sense of greatness and glory. All those marble dudes on their marble horses in grand plazas around the world are the inferior successors to Alexander the Great.

But the Hebrew prophets, being the irascible minstrels of Yahweh that they are, refuse to be impressed with the kind of greatness for which most of us have such a natural predilection. What most of us swoon over, the Hebrew prophets scoff at. The Hebrew prophets are akin to the pigeons in their utter disregard for the dudes on their horses. To this day the poems of the Hebrew prophets mock the slogans and anthems of nationalistic propaganda. In his anti-imperial, countercultural poems the prophet Zechariah imagines an entirely different kind of king as Israel's Messiah—a king that we might describe as the antithesis of Alexander the Great and all the lesser dudes on their lesser horses.

> Rejoice greatly, O daughter of Zion!
> Shout aloud, O daughter of Jerusalem!
> See, your king comes to you;
> triumphant and victorious is he,
> humble and riding on a donkey,
> on a colt, the foal of a donkey.

He will take away the chariot from Ephraim,
and the warhorse from Jerusalem.
The weapons of war will be broken,
and he will teach peace to the nations;
his dominion shall be from sea to sea,
and from the River to the ends of the earth.[9]

In the year 518 BC, while Darius the Great, King of Persia, ruled the world of the Bible and Israel lived in exile, Zechariah penned a poem about an anticipated Jewish king who would someday triumphantly enter Jerusalem, not riding a warhorse, but riding a donkey's colt. This humble king comes not to wage war but to teach peace, to bring an end to war, and to rule the nations "from sea to shining sea." To write a poem like that in the sixth century BC was an audacious act of hope, but it's in times of utter despair that the prophets do their most outlandish acts of hoping against all hope. As Walter Brueggemann says in *The Prophetic Imagination*, "The prophet engages in futuring fantasy. The prophet does not ask if the vision can be implemented, for questions of implementation are of no consequence until the vision can be imagined. The imagination must come before the implementation."[10] In his "futuring fantasy" poem Zechariah speaks of "prisoners of hope."[11] Hope was all the exiles in Babylon had left. So a prophet of hope writes a poem about an imagined Messiah riding a donkey, bringing peace to Jerusalem and ruling the world. A beautiful picture…but it's just a poem, and everyone knows poems don't change the world and crazy daydreams don't come true. So Jerusalem remained under the domination of the Persian Empire. Then the Greek Empire. Then the Roman Empire…until five centuries had passed since Zechariah had written his ludicrous poem of hope. Jerusalem was still not free; all that had changed was the names of Israel's Gentile overlords.

In the spring of (probably) AD 30—547 years after Zechariah's poem—Pontius Pilate arrived in Jerusalem. Pilate ordinarily lived in the Roman city of Caesarea on the Mediterranean coast, but during Passover the Governor of Judea needed to be in Jerusalem to keep order.

Passover—a holiday commemorating Israel's liberation from a foreign empire—was the time when revolts against Roman rule could erupt, and they frequently did. If America was occupied by a foreign power we could assume that the Fourth of July would be a day when civil unrest would be expected. This is what Passover was like during the Roman occupation, so the governor made the seventy-five mile journey to Jerusalem. Coming from Caesarea, Pilate entered the city from the west, riding a horse at the head of the Imperial Calvary. The Roman governor's entrance into Jerusalem was essentially a military parade. It was intended as a show of force to intimidate any would-be revolutionaries. Military parades, then and now, are used by empires to demonstrate that they rule the world through their superior capacity to wage war.

That same week Jesus approached Jerusalem from the east, coming up to the holy city from Jericho accompanied by his twelve disciples and a crowd of Passover pilgrims from Galilee who believed that Jesus was their long-awaited Messiah. This year they came to Jerusalem not only to keep the Passover, but with the anticipation that Jesus would be crowned King of the Jews, launching the revolution that would at last overthrow Rome and usher in the kingdom of God—a revived dynasty of David that would rule the world. As Jesus neared the crest of the Mount of Olives just opposite Jerusalem, he paused and sent two disciples to obtain a donkey's colt from the nearby village of Bethany. Jesus would ride a donkey into Jerusalem, deliberately acting out the ancient poem of Zechariah. Jesus entered Jerusalem from the opposite direction and in the *opposite manner* that Pilate entered the city. Instead of riding on a powerful warhorse like Pilate, Jesus rides a donkey, and not even a full-grown donkey, but a donkey's colt. We can picture the ridiculous sight as Jesus rides a donkey so small that his feet drag the ground. Jesus' triumphal entry was the anti-military parade. It was a mockery of Rome's intimidating show of military power. Imagine a mock military parade where peace protestors are riding tricycles instead of tanks and you get the idea.

But this was a real triumphal entry—the arrival of Israel's true king. This is clearly how the Galilean Passover pilgrims understood it.

As he was now approaching the path down from the Mount of Olives, the whole multitude of the disciples began to praise God joyfully with a loud voice for all the deeds of power that they had seen, saying, "Blessed is the king who comes in the name of the Lord!"[12]

The citizens of Jerusalem were alarmed by this subversive and dangerous street theater staged by Galilean pilgrims with their upstart Messiah. This was the kind of politically charged action that could provoke a violent response from their Roman occupiers. Jerusalem was on edge.

When he entered Jerusalem, the whole city was in turmoil, asking, "Who is this?" The crowds were saying, "This is the prophet Jesus from Nazareth in Galilee."[13]

This was a provocation of the sort Pontius Pilate was in town to prevent. Some observers immediately recognized how dangerous it was and tried to warn Jesus.

Some of the Pharisees in the crowd said to him, "Teacher, order your disciples to stop." He answered, "I tell you, if these keep quiet, the stones will cry out."[14]

This marks the first time that Jesus has allowed himself to be publicly recognized as Israel's Messiah. Until this point whenever someone acknowledged Jesus as the Messianic king, Jesus would charge him to keep quiet. Now that Jesus has come to Jerusalem for his coronation (though he knows it will be by crucifixion), he not only allows a public proclamation of his kingship, he insists that it must be so. This moment—the arrival of Israel's true king—is so auspicious, that if people don't herald it, the rocks will.

Yet Jesus is under no illusion that Jerusalem is going to recognize the arrival of their long-awaited Messianic king. Jerusalem is still looking for a Messiah who is some dude on a horse. Or to speak of it anachronistically, they're looking for their Jewish George Washington. They're looking for a general on a warhorse who holds the reins in one hand and a sword in the other. Jesus is not that. Jesus is riding a donkey and the only weapons his disciples have are palm branches. The Judeans will never recognize this kind of king. So Jesus enters Jerusalem in sorrow.

> As he came near and saw the city, he wept over it, saying, "If you, even you, had only recognized on this day the things that make for peace! But now they are hidden from your eyes. Indeed, the days will come upon you, when your enemies will set up ramparts around you and surround you, and hem you in on every side. They will crush you to the ground, you and your children within you, and they will not leave one stone upon another; because you did not recognize the time of your visitation from God."[15]

After five centuries of waiting, Zechariah's donkey-riding King of Peace had arrived in Jerusalem, but Jerusalem's blind faith in the ways of war made it impossible for them to recognize it. Their expectation of a militant Messiah prevented them from seeing the things that make for peace. Looking for some dude on a horse, Jerusalem missed the Messiah who rode in on a donkey.

What we see on Palm Sunday are two parades. One from the west and one from the east. One where Caesar's Prefect of Judea rides a warhorse and one where God's anointed Messiah rides a donkey. One is a military parade projecting the power of empire—the Roman Empire. The other is a prophetic parade announcing the arrival of an alternative empire—the kingdom of God. One parade derives its power from a willingness to crucify its enemies. The other derives its power by embracing the cross and forgiving its enemies. One is a perpetuation of the domination systems of empire. The other is the only hope the world has for true liberation.

The question is, which parade will we march in? The parade that celebrates empire and militarism and trusts in war to shape the world?

Or the parade that celebrates the Prince of Peace and trusts in God to heal the world? One parade is led by some dude on a horse (or a tank) and those who follow are armed with swords (or combat rifles). The other parade is led by a king on a donkey and those who follow are armed with nothing more deadly than palm branches. The people in each parade think the people in the other parade are persisting in absolute folly—so you'll have to make up your own mind about which parade you want to march in.

Around the same time that Isaiah the son of Amoz was composing his poems about a Prince of Peace and a day when swords would be turned into plowshares, the Greek poet Homer was composing his epic poem *The Iliad.* This six-hundred-page poem about the Trojan War was the closest thing the Greco-Roman world had to a canonical religious text. Its themes are rage, revenge, and war. The poem opens with these lines:

> Rage—Goddess, sing the rage of Peleus' son Achilles,
> murderous, doomed, that cost the Archaeans countless losses,
> hurling down to the House of Death so many sturdy souls,
> great fighters' souls, but made their bodies carrion,
> feasts for dogs and birds,
> and the will of Zeus was moving toward its end.
> Begin, Muse, when the two first broke and clashed,
> Agamemnon lord of men and brilliant Achilles.
> What god drove them to fight with such a fury?[16]

More than 15,000 lines later, the poem ends with these lines:

> Then they collected the white bones of Hector—
> all his brothers, his friends-in-arms, mourning,
> and warm tears came streaming down their cheeks.
> They placed the bones they found in a golden chest,
> shrouding them round and round in soft purple cloths.
> They quickly lowered the chest in a deep, hollow grave

and over it piled a cope of huge stones closely set,
then hastily heaped a barrow, posted lookouts all around
for fear the Achaen combat troop would launch their attack
before the time agreed. And once they'd heaped the mound
they turned back home to Troy, and gathering once again
they shared a splendid funeral feast in Hector's honor,
And so the Trojans buried Hector breaker of horses.[17]

The Iliad begins with rage and ends with a funeral, and in between rivers of blood are shed—all set forth in the most brilliant and beloved poem of the ancient world. The statues of warriors on warhorses are monuments to the kind of martial glory epitomized in The Iliad—the "Bible" of the ancient pagan world. If you're the kind of person who thrills at tales of vengeance-seeking warriors, then Achilles, with his rage and unquenchable lust for revenge, is an iconic hero. Long before there were Clint Eastwood and Charles Bronson movies glorifying revenge, there was The Iliad and the Greek hero Achilles. Though we might want to remember that in The Iliad even the indifferent gods were not entirely pleased when Achilles abused the body of Hector by dragging it behind his chariot.

And so he kept on raging, shaming noble Hector,
but the gods in bliss looked down and pitied Priam's son.[18]

A few years ago I saw the play An Iliad. It's a modern retelling of Homer's Iliad by playwrights Lisa Peterson and Denis O'Hare. The play has only two actors—the Muse (a musician who never speaks) and the Poet. The Poet (probably Homer) is a weary bard, thousands of years old, speaking to a present day audience. Fated to tell his story over and over throughout history, you feel his ancient fatigue. The play is smart, humorous, and wrenching. I was so moved by the performance that I attended it twice, bought tickets for friends, and sent a congratulatory message to Kyle Hatley, the actor who played the demanding role of the Poet. The most moving part of the play for me (and the most difficult part of the script for the actor to memorize) is when the Poet, recalling

the shameful atrocity of Achilles dragging the body of Hector behind his
chariot, says,

> It's so—(*He shakes his head.*)—if you'd see it, the—the
> waste…Just like…(*He blinks, seems to have lost his place.*)
> there was one time…uhhhh…(*Trying to remember.*)… yes
> yes, (*Shakes himself.*)…it was a terrible hot day during the
> Conquest of Sumer—(*He stops to correct himself.*)—I
> mean, the Conquest of Sargon—uh—the Persian war—
> no—

> the Peloponnesian War
> War of Alexander the Great
> Punic War
> Gallic War
> Caesar's invasion of Britain
> Great Jewish Revolt
> Yellow Turban Rebellion
> War Against the Moors in North Africa
> Roman–Persian War
> Fall of Rome
> Byzantine–Arab War
> Muslim Conquest of Egypt
> First Siege of Constantinople
> Arab-Chinese War
> Saxon Wars
> Viking raids across Europe
> Bulgarian Siege of Constantinople
> Zanj Rebellion in southern Iraq
> Croatian–Bulgarian War
> Viking Civil War
> Norman Conquest of England
> First Crusade
> Second Crusade
> Third Crusade

Fourth Crusade
Children's Crusade
Fifth
Sixth
Seventh
Eighth
Ninth Crusade
Norman Invasion of Ireland
Mongol Invasion of China
Mongol Invasion from Russia
Mongol Invasion of Afghanistan
Mongol Invasion of Vietnam
The Hundred Years' War
Chinese Domination of Vietnam
Polish–Lithuanian–Teutonic War
Hunger War
Fall of Constantinople
Wars of the Roses
War of the Priests
Muscovite–Lithuanian Wars
The Spanish Conquest of Mexico
The Mughal Conquest of India
Wars of the Two Brothers
The Spanish Conquest of Peru
Thirty Years' War
Pequot War
First, Second, and Third English Civil Wars
Cromwell's Conquest of Ireland
Cromwell's Conquest of Scotland
The 335 Years' War
The French and Indian Wars
Second Cherokee War
American Revolution
French Revolution
Haitian Revolution

The Napoleonic Wars
The Bolivian War of Independence
Argentine War of Independence
Mexican War of Independence
Bolivian War of Independence
War of 1812
Columbian, Chilean, Peruvian, and Ecuadorian Wars
     of Independence
Lower Canada Rebellion
Upper Canada Rebellion
Second Seminole War
Mormon War
Pastry War
Honey War
First Anglo–Afghan War
First Opium War
The Land Wars
Crimean War
American Civil War
Sioux Wars
Second Anglo–Afghan War
The Boer Wars
Cuban War of Independence
Spanish–American War
Mexican Revolution
World War I
Russian Revolution
Third Anglo–Afghan War
Irish War of Independence
Afghan Civil War
Japanese Invasion of Manchuria
Saudi–Yemeni War
Spanish Civil War
World War II
Palestinian Civil War

Arab–Israeli War
Cold War
Korean War
Cuban Revolution
Tibetan Rebellion
Vietnam
Bay of Pigs
Sand War
Six–Day War
Laos
Cambodia
The Troubles
Prague Spring
Nicaraguan Revolution
Salvadorian Civil War
Soviet Invasion of Afghanistan
Contra War in Nicaragua
Second Sudanese Civil War
The Iran–Iraq War
Falklands War
Israeli Invasion of Lebanon
The First Intifada
The Israeli Invasion of Lebanon
US Invasion of Granada
US Invasion of Panama
First Intifada
Afghan Civil War
Rwandan Civil War
Chechnya
Bosnia and Herzegovina
Chechnya
Afghanistan
Kosovo
Iraq
Chechnya

Afghanistan
Rwanda
Darfur
Iraq
Haiti
Pakistan
Lebanon
Kenya
Zimbabwe
Congo
Gaza
Somalia
Georgia
Iraq
Pakistan
Afghanistan
Libya
Syria...

(The Poet is slumped in the chair, lost.)[19]

At one point in the play the Poet says in utter exhaustion, "Every time I sing this song, I hope it's the last time." Yes, but how is there to be a last time? As Freya Stark has said, "The pendulum of history drips blood at every swing."[20] The first warhorse riders we know of were the warlords of Sumer who galloped across Mesopotamia forty-five centuries ago. In due time warhorses turned into battle tanks and B-2 bombers. But it really is the same thing over and over; it really does seem that the pendulum of history drips blood at every swing. So the weary Poet recites the bloody history: The Conquest of Sumer, The Conquest of Sargon, The Persian war...

And yet Christians celebrate Palm Sunday year after year. Don't we believe that something monumental happened when the King of Kings eschewed the warhorse to ride a peace donkey? Don't we at least believe

Jesus offers us an alternative to all those dudes with their horses, tanks and ICBMs? We must believe it! The Palm Sunday shout is *hosanna!* It means "save now." In a world married to war, now more than ever, we need to acclaim Christ as King and shout hosanna. But our hosanna must not be a plea for Jesus to join our side, bless our troops, and help us win our war—it must be a plea to save us from our addiction to war.

> The King approaches on Palm Sunday
> Forsaking the glorious warhorse
> To ride a ridiculous peace donkey
> Gentle as the wings of a dove
> Inaugurating the reign of love
> Conquerors come with hubris, blood, and violence
> Riding stallions of famine, war, and pestilence
> The Prince of Peace comes without breaking a bruised reed
> Swords are now for plowing, spears are now for pruning
> If *Hosanna* praises rocket's red glare: Weep over Jerusalem
> If *Hosanna* acclaims kingdom come: Let the rocks cry out!

I understand the world is going to have its infatuation for the kind of conquest and militarism symbolized by those dudes-on-horses statues seen in every capital city. But must it be so among those who are heirs of the Hebrew prophets and followers of Jesus of Nazareth? Isn't part of what makes the world the world and not the church, the fact that the world still holds to the old ways of war, while the church follows the king who refused to ride the warhorse? At least isn't it supposed to be that way? One of my deepest concerns for the evangelical church in America is the religious reverence it holds for the ways and means of war. Recently I heard of a Baptist church in Texas that on the Sunday before Memorial Day replaces Christian hymns of worship with the fight songs of the four branches of the military. Instead of singing "Amazing Grace" and "Rock of Ages," they sing "Anchors Aweigh," "The Caissons Go Rolling Along," "The Wild Blue Yonder," and "The Marine's Hymn." Imagine a Baptist church on Sunday morning standing in worship and singing the first verse of "Anchors Aweigh."

Stand, Navy, out to sea, Fight our battle cry;
We'll never change our course, So vicious foe steer shy.
Roll out the TNT, Anchors Aweigh. Sail on to victory
And sink their bones to Davy Jones, hooray![21]

What madness is this? Roll out the TNT?! Sink their bones?!
Hooray?! I can understand this hymn being sung in a Temple of Mars,
but in a church that claims to follow the one who taught us to love our
enemies? Last year when this church sang their war hymns, the Gospel
reading from the Revised Common Lectionary for that Sunday began
with this verse: "Not everyone who says to me, 'Lord, Lord,' will enter
the kingdom of heaven, but only the one who does the will of my
Father in heaven."[22] Amen.

It should be obvious that Jesus is not some dude on a horse; Jesus
did not win his fame in the way of Alexander the Great or George
Washington. Jesus did not, "roll out the TNT." When we see statues of
Jesus, he's not riding a warhorse but dying on a cross. I've never seen a
statue of Jesus riding a horse, though in a church in France I did see a
statue of Jesus riding a donkey. This wooden statue was on wheels; I
assume this was so it could move down the aisle on Palm Sunday. I
would love to see that, though I have to admit it did look a bit silly. But
that's the point, isn't it? The dudes on their horses are oh-so-serious, but
Jesus skewers it all when he rides the two-sizes-too-small donkey on
Palm Sunday. It's because of Jesus that I can poke fun at the dudes-on-
horses statues.

Of course some will ask, what about the white horse rider in the
book of Revelation? In the end doesn't Jesus resort to the ways of war?
No! If God's final solution for violence is simply a more gruesome
version of the Nazi Final Solution, then we might as well throw away
our Bibles away and roll out the TNT. And those caissons go rolling
along. For that matter, if the world is to be shaped by violent power and
not by co-suffering love, we should stop quoting Jesus and start quoting
Nietzsche. If God's solution for evil is to kill people who are evil, God
didn't need to send his Son—he could have just sent in the tanks.

Reading the end of the Bible as though Jesus ultimately renounces the Sermon on the Mount and resorts to catastrophic violence is a reckless and irresponsible reading of the apocalyptic text. I've written elsewhere about how we should read the symbols in the Book of Revelation,[23] but let me just say here that in the metaphorical picture of a triumphant Christ riding a white horse, the rider is drenched in his own blood *before* the battle begins, and the rider whose name is The Word of God prevails with a sword from his mouth, not a sword in his hand. This is how John of Patmos subverts Caesar who, after all, is just another dude on a horse. Jesus does not conquer in the manner of Julius Caesar or Genghis Khan (whose armies killed as many as ten million); Jesus conquers as a slaughtered lamb—by shedding his own blood on the cross and speaking God's word of forgiveness. If you're going to attempt the impossible task of reading Revelation literally, then you have to claim that Jesus is going to ride a flying horse while wearing a stack of crowns and a blood-soaked robe, sporting a "King of Kings" tattoo on his thigh while stabbing millions of people with a sword that he holds— not in his hand—but in his mouth. Of course that's an absurd reading of the text. If we say Jesus isn't *literally* a slaughtered lamb with seven eyes and seven horns, then neither should we say Jesus *literally* rides a flying horse while stabbing people with a mouth sword. There is a far better way of reading Revelation 19.

In his death, burial, resurrection, and ascension, Christ has been elevated to King of Kings. His dominion, Zechariah said, is now from sea to sea and to the ends of the earth. (Zechariah is a prime source for many of John the Revelator's wild images.) In giving my testimony to the saving power of Jesus, I can say that I have seen the white horse and its rider. Indeed, the one on the white horse wears all the crowns! I've been slain by the word that comes from the rider's mouth, and I've been raised to new life. I belong to the armies of heaven who follow the rider called Faithful and True. And though I confess that Christ will come again to judge the living and the dead, I read Revelation 19 as an apocalyptic portrayal of present realities. Christ as a victorious conqueror on a white horse is not something waiting to happen, but a reality that has been ongoing since his resurrection and ascension. For two thousand years the kingdom of Christ has spread across the world by a faithful and true proclamation of the word of God. With his kaleidoscope of metaphors, John reveals what is unseen by those besotted with the world as it is. The blessedness of Revelation is that it reveals a reality that has been unfolding ever since Jesus was exalted to the right hand of God.

"Amen. Come, Lord Jesus! The grace of the Lord Jesus be with all the saints. Amen."[24]

SATAN, YOUR KINGDOM MUST COME DOWN

Satan, your kingdom must come down
Satan, your kingdom must come down
I heard the voice of Jesus say
Satan, your kingdom must come down
— *Traditional*

As a child I wasn't afraid of werewolves, vampires, or Frankenstein monsters, but I was afraid of the devil. Satan was the monster who haunted me—not Satan as a tempter, but Satan as the arch-villain of diabolical evil. The horror movie monsters didn't scare me because I didn't really believe in them, but I believed in the devil. What I was most afraid of was that the devil would suddenly appear—that some day (or more likely some night) I'd open a closet door and suddenly be face to face with Beelzebub, goat horns and all. I assumed that in the infernal encounter I'd drop dead from sheer terror.

I don't remember being taught anything in particular about the devil in church or Sunday school, but like most kids I had picked up a kind of biography of Satan from pop culture and Christian legend that went something like this: Satan had once been Lucifer, the greatest and most beautiful angel, but Lucifer led a rebellion against God, was kicked out of heaven, became the devil, and now has his headquarters in hell from whence he marshals his demons in a great war against God and all that is good. Or something like that. If we ask those who adhere to this account of Satan where this biographical sketch is found in the Bible, we are guided through a cadre of disparate texts beginning with the oracle against the King of Babylon found in Isaiah 14, and especially verse 12 where Isaiah describes the King of Babylon as "Lucifer, son of the morning."[1] But Lucifer doesn't mean Satan (the accuser), it just means Morning Star—a poetic description of the unrivaled majesty of Nebuchadnezzar at the zenith of his power. (Morning Star or Day Star is how most modern translations render the Hebrew word that the King James Version translated as Lucifer—the Latin name for the planet Venus.) So how did the King of Babylon lauded as the Morning Star end up being thought of as the origin of Satan in popular imagination? It's a rather complicated story, and I'll call upon the formidable scholar David Bentley Hart to help explain. In his translation of the New Testament, Hart adds a footnote to 2 Peter 1:19 (a verse which speaks of the morning star rising in Christian hearts), where he explains how Isaiah's "Lucifer" became associated with the popular concept of Satan.

> Phorsphoros, the "Light-Bringer" (Hêlêl in Hebrew, Lucifer in Latin), is the Morning Star (Venus as seen before the dawn). Jesus is also identified with this same "Star of the Morning" at Revelation 22:16. Though later Christian tradition would conflate Isaiah 14:12 (where the fallen King Nebuchadnezzar II of Babylon is apostrophized as Hêlêl ben Shahar, "Lucifer Son of the Morning") and Luke 10:18 (where Christ describes the missions of his disciples as causing Satan to fall from the sky "like lightning"), and thus produce the idea of the fall of "Lucifer" before creation, in the New Testament texts every association with the Morning Star is a good one, and the only person identified as the star "Lucifer" is Christ.[2]

So, in a strictly biblical sense, "Lucifer" has nothing to do with what we call the devil or Satan in Scripture. But despite the confusing fact that the "Lucifer" (Morning Star) of the Old Testament is King Nebuchadnezzar and the "Lucifer" (Morning Star) of the New Testament is Jesus (!), I think there is a way to see Isaiah 14 as connected to what we could properly call satanic and poetically describe as Luciferian.

In Isaiah's prophetic critique of Babylon as a God-defying empire, King Nebuchadnezzar is a personification of the whole imperial project. It's with the aims and ambitions of empire that we encounter one of the primary ways of interpreting the satanic. This is especially true when we connect the satanic with the biblical theme of Babylon. Throughout Scripture Babylon is always darkly associated with the evils of empire. What do I mean by empire? Empires are rich, powerful nations who believe they have a divine right to rule other nations and a manifest destiny to shape history according to their own agenda. Empires want to rule the world. Empires seek a hegemony producing an unholy homogeny—what Hannah Arendt called totalitarianism and what Walter Brueggemann calls totalism. In J.R.R. Tolkien's fertile imagination, this is "the one ring to rule them all" formed by the Dark Lord Sauron in the fires of Mount Doom. (Certainly *The Lord of the Rings* can be read as a tale of heroic resistance to the totalism of inhuman empire.) Empires insist that the only legitimate way of arranging the world is their way. Empires claim that only their hegemonic rule will bring peace to the world. This is the satanic imposter of the peaceable kingdom of God—the *Pax Romana* in opposition to the *Pax Christus.*

In their quest for totalism—where nothing else can be attempted or even imagined—empires become the enemy of God and neighborliness. In the Bible we see God blessing nations in their unique diversity, but always opposing the hegemonic ambitions of empire. Thus Isaiah, Jeremiah, and John the Revelator all tell us that God is opposed to Babylon. The problem with Babylon and all empires is that what they claim for themselves—a divine right to rule other nations and a manifest destiny to shape history—is the very thing God has promised to Messiah.

In Psalm 2 Yahweh gives this magisterial promise to the divinely anointed king: "I will make the nations your heritage, and the ends of the earth your possession."[3] This passage is just one example of many similar messianic passages found throughout the Psalms and Prophets.

As Christians, when we find these Davidic Messianic promises in the Old Testament we instinctively confess that Yahweh's anointed King is the Lord Jesus Christ, so that in the New Testament Jesus is given the supreme title "King of Kings."[4] (Ironically, this title first belonged to King Nebuchadnezzar![5]) In the Apocalypse, John the Revelator depicts Jesus as overcoming the murderous intentions of the dragon (Satan operating through the Roman Empire), ascending to the throne of God, and ruling the nations with a rod of iron.[6]

But empires—then and now—contest the sovereignty of God's Anointed. As the psalmist says,

> The kings of the earth set themselves,
> and the rulers take counsel together,
> against the LORD and his anointed, saying,
> "Let us burst their bonds asunder,
> and cast their cords from us."[7]

Empires with their arrogant aspirations seek to challenge and transgress God's sovereignty. Empires claim for themselves what belongs only to God and his Messiah. Isaiah depicts Babylon's lust for total sovereignty by placing these boastful words in the mouth of King Nebuchadnezzar.

> I will ascend to heaven;
> I will raise my throne
> above the stars of God;
> I will sit on the mount of assembly
> on the heights of Zaphon;
> I will ascend to the top of the clouds,
> I will make myself like the Most High.[8]

"I will be like God!" It's in this sense that Babylon as the archetype of empire and eternal enemy of God can be understood as the kingdom of Satan or what John the Revelator calls the dragon. Outrageous hubris in defiance of God and neighborly love is beastly, dragon-like, satanic.

The urge to empire is an insanity that inevitably drives nations to ruin. In the moment before his descent into madness, King Nebuchadnezzar boasted, "Is this not magnificent Babylon, which I built as a royal capital by my mighty power and for my glorious majesty?"[9] Of course, Nebuchadnezzar didn't build anything—Babylon was built by the cheap labor of the poor. The prophet Daniel had tried to caution the king as he hovered on the brink of insanity, saying, "King Nebuchadnezzar, please accept my advice. Stop sinning and do what is right. Break from your wicked past *and be merciful to the poor.*"[10] But Nebuchadnezzar didn't repent and continued his descent into beastly madness until the holy watcher decreed, "Chop down the tree!"[11] As Nebuchadnezzar was driven from lunacy and human society, eating grass like a beast, his fall was complete. It's given to us as a cautionary tale.

But haughty arrogance leading to insanity is not unique to Babylon, rather it's a template imitated by empires throughout history. According to the *New York Times Magazine*, in 2002 a senior White House advisor told a journalist,

> We're an empire now, and when we act, we create our own reality. And while you're studying that reality—judiciously, as you will—we'll act again, creating other new realities, which you can study too, and that's how things will sort out. We're history's actors …and you, all of you, will be left to just study what we do.[12]

"We're an empire now, and when we act, we create our own reality." Really? Creating "your own reality" could be a textbook definition of insanity. Reality is ontological being—and being is a gift from God. We can no more create our own reality than we can create our own universe. We may *think* we can, but that's a form of insanity. If we fail to understand life as a gracious gift from God, we get a lot of things wrong. When life is viewed as a competitive game of acquisition, the strain to stay on top can lead to pathological anxiety and a litany of foolish decisions. Life is not a game; life is a gift. The purpose of life is not to win; the purpose of life is to learn to love well. Jesus never said,

"Consider the kings and emperors;" Jesus said, "Consider the lilies and the birds." Do this and maybe the rat race won't drive you crazy.

In Isaiah's taunt against Babylon, the empire is condemned for insolence, ruling nations with wrath, employing excessive force, and waging unrelenting persecution against defenseless people. The fall of Babylon results in the earth entering a quiet rest. Even the environment rejoices as natural resources are no longer exploited by the empire.

> But finally the earth is at rest and quiet.
> Now it can sing again!
> Even the trees of the forest—
> the cypress trees and the cedars of Lebanon—
> sing out this joyous song:
> "Since you have been cut down,
> no one will come now to cut us down!"[13]

In its fall Babylon joins the junk heap of has-been empires. In Sheol once-powerful kings and emperors take up the taunt against Babylon.

> In the place of the dead there is excitement over your
> arrival.
> The spirits of world leaders and mighty kings long dead
> stand up to see you.
> With one voice they all cry out,
> "Now you are as weak as we are!"
> Your might and power were buried with you.
> The sound of the harp in your palace has ceased.
> Now maggots are your sheet,
> and worms your blanket.
> How you have fallen from heaven,
> O shining star, son of the morning!"[14]

(When empires fall it's hard for the rest of the world not to gloat.)

Those who see you will stare at you,
and ponder over you:
"Is this the man who made the earth tremble,
who shook kingdoms,
who made the world like a desert
and overthrew its cities,
who would not let his prisoners go home?"[15]

When the ghosts haunting Sheol taunt Babylon by saying it "made the world like a desert," it's reminiscent of what the Roman senator Tacitus recorded in his history of the Roman Empire. Tacitus reports the Celtic chieftain Calgacus making this wry quip: "Rome makes a desert and calls it peace." I assume Calgacus never read Isaiah, but the Hebrew prophet and the Celtic chieftain said the same thing about the propaganda of empire. Turning someone else's homeland into a wasteland is not exactly the same thing as bringing peace. And when Babylon is condemned for not letting prisoners go home, I can't help but think of Guantanamo Bay and child immigration detention centers in Texas. Isaiah's bitter taunt ends with a prophecy that Babylon will soon be swept off the world stage: "I will sweep her with the broom of destruction, says the LORD Almighty."[16] And in 539 BC Babylon fell to Persia. "Babylon is fallen, is fallen," cry the prophets.[17] Nevertheless Babylon has a way of coming back—not the Akkadian-speaking kingdom of southern Mesopotamia, but the satanic dehumanizing spirit of empire. In the days of Jesus that empire was Rome.

In the New Testament we're not given just one Gospel witness to Jesus, but four. The early church resisted the urge to harmonize the four evangelists into a solitary Gospel, choosing instead to wisely maintain four distinctive witnesses. In keeping with their distinctiveness, each of the four Gospels has its own way of introducing Jesus as a public figure.

In Matthew's Gospel, Jesus' public ministry begins with the Sermon on the Mount. Jesus is the prophet like unto Moses reissuing the Torah from a mountaintop. The message is that it is time for a renewed Torah and a renewed Israel.

In Luke's Gospel, Jesus' public ministry is first described as he announced the arrival of Jubilee and the day of divine favor at his hometown synagogue in Nazareth. The message is that it is time for God's favor to fall upon all people.

In John's Gospel, Jesus begins his public ministry by turning water into wine at the wedding feast in Cana. The message is that it is time for the long-awaited feast of God to begin.

In Mark's Gospel, the first of the four Gospels to be written, Jesus begins his public ministry by casting out a demon at the synagogue in Capernaum. The message is that it is time for the overthrow of Satan's kingdom. *Satan, your kingdom must come down.*

Mark gives more attention to Jesus' work of casting out demons than any other Gospel writer—Mark sees much of Jesus' ministry as a confrontation with the kingdom of Satan. Jesus' single message was the arrival of the kingdom of God—everything Jesus ever taught or did was an announcement or an enactment of the new government arriving on earth from heaven. It's in the synagogue in Capernaum where Jesus first throws down the gauntlet and proclaims, "Satan, your kingdom must come down!" But the satanic empire strikes back and immediately Jesus faces a sinister challenge from the powers of darkness.

> Suddenly, a man in the synagogue who was possessed by an evil spirit began shouting, "Why are you interfering with us, Jesus of Nazareth? Have you come to destroy us? I know who you are—the Holy One sent from God!"[18]

Why does the demon describe what Jesus is doing as "interfering with us"? Because Jesus is announcing the arrival of a new kingdom—and ultimately there are only two kingdoms, the kingdom of the world ruled by Satan (the god and ruler of the fallen world) and the kingdom of God ruled by Christ.[19] Everything Jesus said and did was an interference with Satan's kingdom including the whole world of dehumanizing empire. The dragon's kingdom of beastly empire (to borrow from the images of Revelation) is built on rivalry, accusation, violence, and domination. We see this played out in the biblical account of the rise of human civilization—the story of Cain and Abel.

When dangerous rivalry first emerged, threatening the relationship between humanity's first two brothers—the farmer and the herdsman—Cain was warned by God, "Sin is crouching at your door; it desires to have you, but you must rule over it."[20] Tragically, Cain did not win the struggle with sin but was overcome by the satanic as he refused to acknowledge Abel as brother and himself as his brother's keeper. Instead Cain considered Abel not his brother but other and enemy. Cain began to accuse Abel in his own mind, eventually plotting his murder. The first murder was not a crime of passion but premeditated. Satan had built a stronghold in the imagination of Cain.

In an attempt to understand what the Bible is trying to communicate about Satan, we should keep in mind that Satan is not a proper name and really should be rendered as "the satan." Satan is simply the un-translated Hebrew word for accuser. Thus in Zechariah 3:1 we are told that "the satan" stood up to "satan" Joshua (that is, the accuser stood up to accuse Joshua). The same is true for the Greek *diabolos* (devil)—it too means accuser. Though we are accustomed to treating "satan" as a proper name, this is a result of popular custom and not something found in the biblical text. What we should take away from the use of the word "satan" and "devil" is that accusation, blame, and slander are the essence of the satanic and diabolical. The Holy Spirit is the spirit of advocacy—the unholy spirit is the spirit of accusation.

After succumbing to the temptations of rivalry and accusation, Cain lured his brother into a field where he attacked and killed him. Rivalry and accusation leading to violence—this is the satanic. After being banished into the land of Nod east of Eden, Cain founded the first city, and from this first city came the later empires of domination—Egypt, Assyria, Babylon and the rest. Rivalry, accusation, violence, domination, culminating in beastly empire—this is the trajectory of the satanic.

But beginning in Galilee Jesus of Nazareth preached the arrival of a new empire—the empire of God. Alarmed by the proclamation of God's kingdom, the demon in the Capernaum synagogue asked Jesus,

"Have you come to destroy us?" The gospel answer is, "Yes!" As the Apostle John wrote, "The Son of God appeared for this purpose, to destroy the works of the devil."[21] The kingdom of God is built on all that the kingdom of Satan is opposed to. Instead of rivalry, there is to be love. Instead of accusation, there is to be advocacy. Instead of violence, there is to be peace. Instead of domination, there is to be liberation. Instead of maintaining the vicious cycle of beastly empire, Jesus comes to establish the humane kingdom come from heaven. This is the gospel! The demonic is all that is negation, pro-death, and anti-human. Jesus brings all that is flourishing, life-affirming, and truly pro-life.

So Jesus rebuked the demon and cast it out. The war against Satan had begun and Jesus had won a battle in the synagogue of Capernaum. Yet the man was not destroyed; the man was liberated, healed, and restored. Jesus overthrows satanic empire, not by violent revolution, but by the power of the Holy Spirit, by establishing the kingdom of God in a world once ruled by Satan. The downfall of Satan's kingdom is the undeniable sign of kingdom come—as Jesus said, "If it is by the Spirit of God that I cast out demons, then the kingdom of God has come to you."[22]

If we are to be faithful disciples of Jesus, we must join our King in his campaign to overthrow Satan's kingdom. But how are we to understand the satan? Is the satan a fallen angel? Certainly the satanic is the fallenness of all that is beautiful and noble. But is the devil an actual *personage*? I think the answer is…almost. I understand the devil as more than a metaphor, but less than a person; the devil is a phenomenon— but a phenomenon so complex that it verges on self-awareness. Consider hurricanes. Hurricanes are meteorological phenomena; they are highly organized and extremely dangerous weather systems. We are so in awe of their destructive power that we personify them by giving them names. Camille, Hugo, Andrew, Katrina. Naming hurricanes doesn't mean we believe there is a person in the sky named Katrina wreaking havoc on New Orleans. But if we say Katrina isn't a person, *that doesn't mean Katrina doesn't exist!* Katrina very much exists and she is very dangerous. But hurricanes are simple compared to Satan. Hurricanes are weather systems formed by moist warm air, the rotation of the earth, and a few other relatively simple factors. The satanic, on the other hand, is generated from the greatest complexity we know anything about—the complexity of the human psyche and human social structures. Out of human anxiety, rivalry, rage, and blame, the devil is born.

The devil has real existence...to a point. It seems that the phenomenon of the satanic is so real, so complex, so organized, that it almost comes into its own ontological existence. But alas, this is the limitation of evil—evil does not possess positive existence, only negation. As Augustine suggested, evil is only a hole in the fabric of goodness. And as Stanley Hauerwas says, "that is why the devil is at once crafty but self-destructively mad, for the devil cannot help but be angry, recognizing as he must that he does not exist."[23] But in saying that the devil is a spiritual and sociological phenomenon—more than a metaphor, less than a person—*let no one say I don't believe the devil is real!* Of course I believe the devil is real! The devil is more real than Hurricane Katrina that (who?) claimed 1,833 lives. It's true—"the devil prowls around like a roaring lion, seeking someone to devour."[24]

So why do I make a point of somewhat demythologizing the devil? I do so only out of pastoral concern. If a Christian can go her whole life believing in the devil as a literal person and have no theological problems with that, I have no inclination to change her mind. But as a pastor I have met too many people who are theologically troubled by the mythological notion of a personal Satan. Sometimes their theological troubles are put as simply as this: "If all our woes are because of the devil, why doesn't God just kill the devil?" Good question. Years ago I heard a famous preacher say, "If I were God, the first thing I'd do is kill the devil. Then I'd invite all the demons to his funeral and kill them too." Behind the levity of this quip there lurks some serious theological conundrums. Why *doesn't* God just destroy the (d)evil? Because the satanic phenomenon is inextricably connected with who we are. God cannot simply destroy the devil in one fell blow without destroying us too. Jesus came to destroy the devil, but the devil will not be destroyed like Osama Bin Laden was destroyed by Seal Team Six. It takes more than a bullet to the head to kill the devil. Jesus destroys the devil by calling us out of rivalry, accusation, violence, domination, and empire, into heaven's alternative of love, advocacy, peace, and liberation—this is what the Bible calls the kingdom of God.

So, yes, I believe the devil is real. Not in the way I believed as a child when I was afraid I might find the devil leaping out of my closet with pitchfork and pointed tail—no, I believe the devil is much *more* real than that. The devil is the all too real dark spiritual phenomenon of accusation and empire that lies behind humanity's greatest crimes—the crucifixion of Jesus Christ, the medieval crusades conducted in his name, the lynching of black men in the Jim Crow South, and the murder of six million Jews in the Holocaust. The devil is also very real in a million smaller, yet still diabolical, acts of rivalry, accusation, violence, and domination that take place every day. Ultimately the Satan reaches its fullest form in the evils of empire. But the good news is that Christ has overthrown the kingdom of Satan with the establishment of his own empire—an Easter Empire.

When Abraham left Ur he was searching for a city—an alternative to the kind of civilization created by Cain. The writer of Hebrews says Abraham was searching for "the city that has foundations, whose architect and builder is God."[25] Abraham was looking for a city not built on the buried bodies of innocent Abels. Human history, shaped by empires and the wars that form and sustain them, creates a reality for most human beings that Thomas Hobbes in his book *Leviathan* (named after a biblical beast) famously described as one of living in continual fear and danger of violent death, where human life is solitary, poor, nasty, brutish, and short.[26] But why is it so? Why are we constrained to live in dread of violent death? In the American war film *The Thin Red Line*, Private Edward Train raises the question in a whispered prayer.

> This great evil—where's it come from? How'd it steal into the world? What seed, what root did it grow from? Who's doing this? Who's killing us? Robbing us of life and light. Mocking us with the sight of what we might have known.[27]

"Who's doing this?" If we answer, "them," while pointing our finger at vilified others, we fail to recognize that the vilified "them" are just as confidently pointing an accusatory finger at us. And a wicked grin creeps over the devil's face. Who's doing this? When properly understood as the complex phenomenon of accusation and empire, the best answer to this dark question is...Satan. Throughout history civilization has been organized around the power to kill—by empires who weaponize the ways and means of death. It's the legacy bequeathed by Cain, and it seems the human race has been incapable of imagining anything else...until Easter.

Easter is the door opened by Christ that leads to a world beyond the brutality of the Leviathan, beyond the thin red line of bloody battle, beyond a world under the domination of Satan. And no one has captured the idea of Easter as the inauguration of a new world better than G.K. Chesterton. Just as Orthodox Christians always quote from Chrysostom's Paschal homily on Easter, I cannot let Easter come and go without quoting this poignant passage from Chesterton's *Everlasting Man*.

> On the third day the friends of Christ coming at daybreak to the place found the grave empty and the stone rolled away. In varying ways they realized the new wonder; the world had died in the night. What they were looking at was the first day of a new creation, with a new heaven and a new earth; and in a semblance of a gardener God walked again in the garden, in the cool not of the evening but the dawn.[28]

So what does it mean that in the resurrection of Christ an old world has died and a new world has dawned? It means we now have a world of new possibilities. My proposal to the Western church of the 21st century—the heirs of a now defunct Christendom—is to participate in the overthrow of the kingdom of Satan by reclaiming the resurrection as the announcement and embrace of the new way of being human inaugurated by Jesus Christ and his Easter Empire. And make no mistake about it, it is a *re*-claiming of resurrection. Since the catastrophe of Constantine and the emergence of the imperial church seventeen centuries ago, Easter and Christianity have been commandeered to serve the interests of empire. Though Christendom as a viable project is mostly dead, its ghost still haunts the aspirations of post-Christian superpowers. As the horrors of the Trump administration's policy of separating children from asylum-seeking parents apprehended at the United States border and placing these children in separate detention camps fell under heavy criticism, Attorney General Jeff Sessions attempted to defend the abhorrent practice by saying, "I would cite to you the Apostle Paul and his clear and wise command in Romans 13, to obey the laws of the government because God has ordained the government for his purposes."[29] But the top Justice Department official failed to cite the tenth verse of Romans 13 where the Apostle Paul says, "Love does no wrong to a neighbor; therefore, love is the fulfilling of the law." Love that fulfills the law looks like welcoming the stranger, not taking away their kids and imprisoning the traumatized children in detention camps. But the last thing an empire wants is a risen Christ judging its anti-life policies and practices. So measures must be taken.

> Pilate said to them, "You have a guard of soldiers; go, make it as secure as you can." So they went with the guard and made the tomb secure by sealing the stone.[30]

The tomb of Jesus must be made secure by Roman soldiers because empires are always obsessed with security—it's the one thing that is truly sacred. In my travels around the world I've visited many holy sites where I was required to remove my shoes—Hindu temples, Buddhist temples, Moslem mosques, and even some Christian churches in India. But the only place I'm required to remove my shoes in America is at airport security—in our secular age, security may be the only thing America holds sacred. Pontius Pilate would understand this way of thinking. The Roman governor was tasked with maintaining the status quo and keeping the world unchanged, so soldiers were dispatched and an imperial seal was affixed to the tomb of Jesus. By imperial decree the dead are to stay dead! But unbeknownst to Emperor Tiberius or Governor Pilate the old order where death has the final say had passed away.

Now after the Sabbath, toward the dawn of the first day of the week, Mary Magdalene and the other Mary went to see the tomb. And behold, there was a great earthquake, for an angel of the Lord descended from heaven and came and rolled back the stone and sat on it. His appearance was like lightning and his clothing white as snow. And for fear of him the guards trembled and became like dead men.[31]

Do you see it? Do you see what has happened? Do you see the great reversal of the world order? A single angel comes from heaven and defies the security apparatus of soldiers and seals, of Tiberius and Pilate. The angel rolls back the stone, breaking the imperial seal and revealing a new world order—an order no longer arranged around death. "The guards trembled and became like dead men." The once-dead man in the tomb is no longer dead, and those who formerly used the fear of death to shape the world now tremble and become like dead men. The fear-mongers are afraid and the death-dealers are dead. Everything is reversed! The angel tells the two Marys to "fear not" and then escorts them over the "dead" soldiers to see the empty tomb. The soldiers aren't really dead (because heaven doesn't use the banished weapon of death), but the old way of arranging the world is dead and the kingdom of Satan is coming down. This is Easter.

Of course, we have to believe and live our way into this new Easter reality. This is the real-life hard work of being formed as truly Christian people. It's what the Apostle Paul is talking about when he says, "We walk by faith, not by sight."[32] We must hear heaven say, "Fear not," see an empty tomb, and then go with joy to announce the good news of the Orthodox Paschal hymn,

> Christ is risen from the dead,
> Trampling down death by death,
> And on those in the tombs bestowing life!

If indeed death is undone and fear is no longer the deciding factor, then we are near the border of a new land where all things are possible. A Christianity untethered from imperial compromise is free to imagine new Easter possibilities. In the morning light of Easter, the totalism of Satan is overthrown and the followers of the Lamb hear the one seated on the throne say, "Behold, I am making all things new."[33]

CHAPTER 8
FEEL THE FALSENESS

The first precondition of being called a spiritual leader is to perceive and feel the falsehood that is prevailing in society, and then to dedicate one's life to a struggle against that falsehood. If one tolerates the falsehood and resigns oneself to it, one can never become a prophet. If one cannot rise above material life, one cannot even become a citizen in the Kingdom of the Spirit, far less a leader of others.
—*Vladimir Solovyov in his eulogy of Fyodor Dostoevsky, 1881*

The Russian poet and philosopher Vladimir Solovyov eulogized Fyodor Dostoevsky as a prophet precisely because Dostoevsky could feel the falseness prevailing in society. Dostoevsky could see through the lies that the masses agreed to believe. Dostoevsky's greatest novels—*Notes From Underground, Crime and Punishment, The Idiot, Demons, The Brothers Karamazov*—were artistic masterpieces of prophetic truth-telling. What most people were too obtuse, too compromised, or just too afraid to see, Dostoevsky set forth in his novels—they were parables writ large (very large!). Why was Dostoevsky able to perceive and portray so clearly the falseness that pervaded Russian society in the waning days of the czars? I'm not entirely sure. Dostoevsky had a deep Christian faith, but he was far from a saint—he struggled most of his life with a gambling addiction that often drove him to the brink of ruin. Perhaps it was related to his extraordinary novelistic gift. The greatest writers of fiction always tell the truth with unflinching honesty! The one thing a great writer of fiction must not do is to tell his tale untruthfully.

Dostoevsky could write so convincingly about the gambler Alexei Ivanovich, the buffoon Fyodor Karamazov, the murderer Rodion Raskolnikov, and the unnamed underground man with his dark neuroses because he knew the potential to be a great sinner lurked within himself. Indeed the novel Dostoevsky was preparing to write at the time of his death was a sequel to *The Brothers Karamazov* entitled *The Life of A Great Sinner*. Having felt the potential for falseness in his own soul, Dostoevsky was humble enough and wise enough to feel it in society. Whatever kind of sinner Dostoevsky was, he wasn't a hypocrite, and this enabled him to perceive and write important things in powerful ways.

Dostoevsky did his writing during the end of an epoch. For centuries Russia had been ruled by Christian czars with the support of the Orthodox Church, but within a generation of his death the Bolshevik Revolution brought it all to a bloody end, inaugurating the Soviet era—a catastrophe that Dostoevsky seemed to foresee and foretell in his novel *Demons*. Dostoevsky understood that a society so saturated in falseness, no matter how Christian, could not continue to endure. A house of cards or a house built on sand cannot stand forever. A society that has long been the heir of Christian legacy can easily forget that it is not by merely *knowing* the words of Christ, but by actually *doing* them that a Christian society stands upon a sure foundation. Jesus warns us about this with these sobering words:

> And everyone who hears these words of mine and does not act on them will be like a foolish man who built his house on sand. The rain fell, and the floods came, and the winds blew and beat against that house, and it fell—and great was its fall![1]

This is my question for you, dear reader, "Can you feel it?" It's all around you, but can you *feel* it? Can you feel the falseness that prevails in Babylon? Babylon is always religious and knows how to keep up appearances, but that only serves to conceal the idols Babylon really worships. Money and Power. Economy and Military. The falseness is the phony assumption that the pursuit of money and power is sustainable and leads to a life worth living. In the Babylon in which I reside (hopefully as a missionary) the falseness is very strong right now—stronger than it's ever been in my life. But most people are so sedated with the opiates of consumer culture and consumer religion that they never even suspect it. There are others who sense it but cannot quite name it. It takes a prophet to name it. It takes the courage of a prophet to come right out and call materialism and militarism a lie. Jesus was that kind of prophet. Listen to these bracing words spoken not to antagonistic Pharisees but to those in the capital city of Jerusalem "who had believed in him."

> You are from your father the devil, and you choose to do your father's desires. He was a murderer from the beginning and does not stand in the truth, because there is no truth in him. When he lies, he speaks according to his own nature, for he is a liar and the father of lies. Because I tell you the truth, you do not believe me.[2]

This is what Jesus told the Judeans who purported to believe in him but still clung to the idea that freedom is attained by the murderous ways of Cain. The Judean disciples boasted of their freedom while Jesus insisted they were slaves to sin.[3] They wanted to claim they believed in Jesus, but they also wanted to believe they could kill for the sake of "freedom" and still call themselves the children of Abraham. But they were not children of Abraham; Jesus said they were children of the devil, the offspring of Cain. Cain was the devil-inspired original murderer who killed his brother for the sake of money, power, manifest destiny, and a perverted concept of freedom. In conversing with these freedom-loving faux disciples Jesus felt the falseness of their faith and called it what it was—the lies and desires of the devil! The Judean disciples didn't like being confronted with their falseness "so they picked up stones to throw at him, but Jesus hid himself and went out of the temple."[4] Six months later Jesus was back in Jerusalem again exposing the falseness.

> For this purpose I was born and for this purpose I have
> come into the world—to bear witness to the truth.
> Everyone who is of the truth listens to my voice.[5]

Pilate's cynical reply is infamous. "What is truth?"[6] After having
Jesus scourged, Pilate answered his own question about truth when he
said to Jesus, "Do you not know that I have power to release you, and
power to crucify you?"[7] This is Pilate's truth, Caesar's truth, Cain's truth,
Satan's truth—the will to shape the world by violent power. For the
"great men of the world," ultimate truth is the power to kill. Even the
High Priest Caiaphas is complicit in this lie when he confesses, "We
have no king but Caesar."[8] Imagine the moment when the Jewish high
priest removes his religious mask and admits that his ultimate allegiance
is pledged to a pagan emperor! What a stunning betrayal of everything
the Hebrew prophets stood for! In the Roman Empire, power trumps
everything and the high priest is along for the ride. The high priest can
hold prayer breakfasts to maintain the façade, but long ago he sold his
soul for a seat at the table of imperial power.

In an economic-military superpower, the truth is that money and
power trump everything. That's the truth that is the lie. That's the
functional atheism of religious people who pretend at faith but bow the
knee to Mammon and Mars. That's the falseness that prevails. That's the
deception of a material society. Can you feel it? The great lie is that life
is about the acquisition of money and other forms of power. The grand
deceit is that in the pursuit of wealth and power all means are justified.
Every war is justified if it's for the sake of The Economy. The lie is that
to live the abundant life you have to have proximity to power—
especially the power to kill. In Babylon this lie is pervasive, persuasive,
and seductive…as idolatry always is.

But can you feel the falseness of it all? Don't you realize that even if
the idolatry of materialism and militarism is preached beneath steeples
and ensconced behind stained-glass it's still antichrist? Resist it! Don't
tolerate it! Rise above it! Cain was wrong and his city was built on a lie.
The meaning of life is not about besting your brother, beating your
brother, conquering your brother, killing your brother. Life is about

caring for your brother. That's not naiveté, that's Christianity! Nietzsche was wrong. The meaning of life is not found in power, the meaning of life is found in love. God is not totalized will to power, God is kenotic self-sacrificing love. Yet far too many Christians who profess to be appalled at Nietzsche's axiom, "God is dead," seem enthralled by Nietzsche's Will To Power. When American Christians tacitly agree with Nietzsche and openly agree with Ayn Rand, you know that something has gone horribly wrong—the falseness has become malignant.

So let us not talk falsely now, the hour is getting late. Let's remember again the radical profession that we Christians make. We confess that Jesus is the world's true king. We confess that Jesus is Lord…right now. The rightful ruler of the world is not some ancient Caesar, not some contemporary Commander in Chief, but Jesus Christ! Jesus is not going to be king someday, Jesus is King of Kings *right now!* Christ was crowned on the cross and God vindicated him as the world's true king by raising him from the dead. This is what Christians confess, believe, and seek to live. We have no king but Jesus. And our king has nothing to do with violent power. Our king has no use for nuclear weapons. Why? Because you can't love your neighbor with hydrogen bombs. Our king said his kingdom does not come from the world of war, which is why his servants do not fight. Jesus told Pontius Pilate, "My kingdom is not from this world. If my kingdom were from this world, my servants would be fighting."[9] The kingdom from heaven that Jesus brings into the world does not come riding an M1 Abrams tank. In the kingdom of the Prince of Peace, we study war no more, we turn swords into plowshares and spears into pruning hooks, we turn tanks into tractors and missile silos into grain silos. Our task is not to turn the world into a battlefield, our task is to turn the world into a garden. Our goal is not Armageddon, our goal is New Jerusalem. *We're marching to Zion, the beautiful city of God.*

Of course Governor Pilate doesn't believe any of this. And neither does the billionaire King Herod. The faith leader Caiaphas will give some lip service to this, because it's in the Bible, but the faith leader will kick the can down the road saying, "All that peace stuff is for when the Messiah comes, but for now it's all about power; for now we have no king but Caesar; for now proximity to power trumps everything." What Caiaphas wants most of all is access to the most powerful man in the world. Caiaphas wants an invitation to the imperial palace, a trip to the White House, an Oval Office photo-op. How pathetic. These fake faith leaders can't feel the falseness, they *are* the falseness! When we see faith leaders fawning over proximity to political power, don't we feel the falseness of their faith? Don't we know that they too have secretly confessed, "We have no king but Caesar"? "Woe to them! For they go the way of Cain, and abandon themselves to Balaam's error for the sake of gain."[10]

Again I ask, can you feel the falseness? I hope you can. If you can, it means you have a heart for the truth. Keep feeding that holy desire. "Buy the truth, and do not sell it."[11] Trust the holy instincts within you—the instincts of compassion aroused by the Holy Spirit. Yes, politics are always complicated, but what does Jesus want your attitude to be toward Syrian refugees, Honduran asylum seekers, and undocumented day laborers? You already know. You've always known. Some will say power trumps everything, but you've always known that mercy triumphs over judgment. Hold on to what you know to be true and don't be talked out of it by compromised faith leaders.

Yet many simple souls are being led astray. The evidence is all around us. Consider this question: Should a follower of Jesus support torture under *any* circumstance? You know the answer to that too. But when a 2014 *Washington Post*/ABC News poll revealed that a majority of white evangelicals in America support the use of torture by the CIA,[12] you know there is a great falseness prevailing within that particular religious subculture. Evangelical support of torture is an "eruption of the real." It's a horrifying moment of unintended truth-telling where we discover that allegiance to national self-interest and the idol of "security" trumps allegiance to Jesus Christ. When you support illegal torture by secret police over the Sermon on the Mount, what does it mean to claim you're a Christian? In light of this, how can we say that evangelicalism in white America is anything other than a failed experiment? When more than half of the adherents of a Christian movement cannot identify torture as immoral, what is there left to say?

But how does such a deception take hold? It happens when spiritual leaders who cannot rise above the material life capitulate to the machinations of empire. And it happens when people assume that God is on their side regardless of what they do. When that assumption prevails, all critical and moral assessment is abandoned; all that matters is what we think benefits the prosperity and security of "our side." As Bob Dylan pointed out, "You never ask questions when God's on your side." But *Gott Mit Uns*[13] has more than a dubious history. There's nothing more false than *Gott Mit Uns* when the task at hand is to kill all your enemies.

In the context of an economic-military superpower, I see no warrant for believing God's people will be the political majority—not until the Parousia anyway. In this present age, if we're unwilling to live as a counter-imperial counterculture (as the first Christians did), I see no reason to believe that we can live in fidelity to Christ. In an economic-military superpower, it's only by acquiescing to the falseness that Christians can hold political dominance. So let go of that seductive aspiration. We don't need to grasp for "the kingdoms of the world and their glory."[14] We can live as responsible citizens as we seek to bear prophetic witness to the rulers, calling them to compassion and justice, but we will not sell our soul for the sake of political power. We're not called to win but to be faithful. When we adopt a win-at-all-cost approach to our participation in partisan politics, the cost may be our soul—our Christian authenticity.

Politics is the art of compromise, but there are some areas where Christians must not compromise. You can't absolve the sin of being pro-torture by claiming to be pro-life. If making America great again involves waterboarding, nuclear weapons, child detention camps, and ridiculing environmental concerns, it's a project Christians cannot participate in. When Joshua met the angel of the Lord and asked, "Are you for us or for our enemies?" the angel replied, "Neither."[15] It's a hard lesson to learn, but Joshua learned it—we cannot assume that God is on our side; rather we can only seek to be on God's side. So at the end of his life Joshua said to the congregation of Israel:

> Choose this day whom you will serve, whether the gods
> your ancestors served in the region beyond the River or
> the gods of the Amorites in whose land you are living; but
> as for me and my household, we will serve the LORD.[16]

The falseness that prevails pretends we can serve the gods of
nationalism *and* the Lord Jesus Christ, but it's a lie. Joshua's ancient swan
song sermon still challenges us today: Choose this day whom you will
serve. The question cannot be truly answered by glibly mouthing, "We
will serve the Lord." In the rising tide of nationalism, the test is how
Christians live and what they're willing to support in the name of
nationalism. In 1930s Germany, the majority of Protestants failed the test.
That's not a cheap shot at Christian nationalism, but a sober warning.

The attempt to simultaneously serve the gods of nationalism and
the Lord Jesus Christ has its most public origin with the Emperor
Constantine. But how Constantine lived his Christianity is quite
revealing. In delaying his baptism for twenty-five years—until he was
nearing death—what was Constantine saying? Wasn't he saying that he
couldn't really be a Christian until he was dead? Wasn't he saying that
ultimately his Christian faith was for the afterlife and not for this
present life? And wouldn't Jesus and the Apostles call that an enormous
falseness? Jesus didn't preach a gospel for the dead; Jesus preached a
gospel for the living and said, "Let the dead bury their own dead."[17]
When Jesus commissioned his disciples to proclaim the kingdom of
God, he did not mean for them to say, "The kingdom of God is at
hand, but don't worry about any radical changes—for now we're going
to keep on fighting and striving and killing for greatness like we always
have." Yet when I preach the gospel of the kingdom by announcing (as
the early church did) that we are now living in the eschaton of the
Prince of Peace, someone always drags out Ecclesiastes to tell me there's
"a time to kill and a time to heal, a time to love and a time to hate, a
time for war and a time for peace,"[18] by which they mean, "now is not
the time to heal, love, and make peace; now is the time to kill, hate, and
wage war." But do you feel the falseness? If we as Christians divide

history into BC and AD, but claim that it's still the time to kill, hate, and wage war, we've made a mockery of our faith! We can't claim to be Christians while wanting to live in the time before Christ.

So let us recover our courage. Let us dare to live a risky Christianity. Let us dare to be a counterculture pushing back against the falseness prevailing in society. Let us risk being ridiculed, mocked, or worse. Let us not play it safe. Jesus never promised us safety. Jesus promised us abundant life, eternal life, true life—but Jesus never promised us a safe life. In my time of dying I doubt I'll find any comfort in having played it safe, but I will find comfort in being able to honestly say that I chose a risky live for the sake of the kingdom of Christ. If you feel the falseness prevailing in society, then reject the falseness by risking everything on the gamble that what the Gospels say about Jesus Christ is true.

The Last Train Out of Monkeytown

He caught the last train out of Monkeytown
Bought a ticket on Easter 04 and was eastbound
Left the wagon train beamed from outer space
Said adios to the obtuse and turned his face
Toward something he hoped was there

Was it the Conductor's last call
With a shudder he sometimes wonders
What would have happened had he missed that train
He fears he'd have shrunk smaller and smaller
Until he disappeared
Not entirely invisible, but totally unrecognizable
To who he was supposed to be
The one he still hopes to become

Curiosity may have killed some cat
But not this cat
For this cat curiosity was a saving grace
Salvation from the dismal fate of the incurious
The Last Man who invents happiness
Or so he thinks
While he sits on his couch
(With seven hundred channels)
And stupidly blinks

That curious cat will tell you
Age may steal your good looks and jump shot
But don't let it abscond with your curiosity
What's the point of living four score
If you know it all in the first score
Don't sit there until the raven croaks nevermore
A world of wonder lies behind an untried door

Truth is not a laminated card you carry in your pocket
Truth is a long hard road and you have to walk it
And you might as well know it's a toll road too
You *will* be required to sacrifice your certitude
But that's okay, it's only a small pittance
To bid good riddance to a dead end existence

Was it a train he caught or road he walked
Seems the metaphors got mixed
Oh well
Whether he hit the road or rode the rails
He thanks God for the grace to bid farewell
To the backwaters of Monkeytown
For a journey through dark heat
To a new dawn of becoming
Becoming
Becoming

CHAPTER 9

TRUMPED

Politics trumps everything. That's an axiom that holds up. Unless you really see the kingdom of God and are willing to rethink everything in the light of Christ, politics trumps everything—including faith and ethics. I learned this the hard way. When I pulled away from lock-step allegiance with the Religious Right because I had seen the kingdom of God and had begun to take Jesus and the Sermon on the Mount seriously, many politically conservative Christians accused me of "going over to the other side." Committed as they were to a dualistic us vs. them paradigm, they could only interpret my kingdom-conscious approach to politics as traitorous. "If you're not on *our* side, you must be on *their* side!" In their closed dualistic system, even Jesus has to be either a Republican or a Democrat. So my honest claim to have no interest in the Left/Right political divide because I only cared about following Jesus fell on deaf ears. They could not see the kingdom alternative I was pointing to—they could only see us vs. them, Republicans vs. Democrats, Elephants vs. Donkeys. They were incredulous about my claim to only be interested in following the Lamb. Yes, I learned the hard way that if the kingdom of Christ is not perceived as a viable alternative society, then competition for conventional political power seems the only option for influencing the world. With a low ecclesiology, politics trumps everything. If the local church is viewed as devoid of what we think of as real power, then we inevitably set our sights on Washington D.C. The National Prayer

Breakfast is believed to be important, not because of prayer, but because the President and other power brokers are there. And once you're convinced that God is working through the political machinations of Babylon, and that God is inviolably on the side of *your* political party...well, you have set yourself up to make enormous compromises. So let me talk about the elephant in the room—Donald J. Trump.

Thus far in this book I have only briefly mentioned Donald Trump, though I have repeatedly talked about and critiqued Christian nationalism. And in the current American context, to talk about Christian nationalism is to talk about Donald Trump. I take the widely reported 81 percent support of Donald Trump among white evangelicals to be primarily driven by the aims of Christian nationalism. Christian Trumpism and Christian nationalism are essentially synonymous. Of course the subject of Donald Trump is as volatile as the man himself, and I want to tread as carefully and speak as precisely as possible. So let me tell a personal story pertaining to Donald Trump and Christian faith that is entirely removed from the present political context.

In January 2011 my book *Unconditional?: The Call of Jesus to Radical Forgiveness* was published. This book is my attempt to present on a popular level a substantive theology of Christian forgiveness. Noted theologian and Yale Professor of Theology Miroslav Volf wrote the foreword. Though it's written for a popular audience, I regard it as a serious book on the theology of forgiveness. My charismatic publishing company had surprisingly chosen to make *Unconditional?* their featured new release, and considerable promotion was placed behind the book. I did book signings at bookseller's conventions, gave dozens of print and radio interviews, and appeared on several Christian television networks, including TBN and Daystar. I was delighted to talk about Jesus' message of radical forgiveness in these popular forums. But when my publicist scheduled me to appear on the Paula White show to promote *Unconditional?*, I balked. Televangelist Paula White represents the most egregious form of the American prosperity gospel—a distortion of the gospel so extreme that it can only be described as aberrant. So I informed my publisher that I would not appear on Paula White's show—my conscience would not allow me to be associated with that kind of Americanized, glamorized, "you-can-have-it-all," health-and-wealth consumer Christianity.

I thought my decision to decline this appearance would be the end of the matter, but it was not. I received a phone call from the executive vice-president of the publishing company urging me to go on the show. Paula White is extremely popular with a massive television audience, and my appearance on her show would doubtless be an enormous boost to book sales. Nevertheless, I told her I would not do it. A few hours later, I received a call from the founder and CEO of the publishing company who said, "Look, Brian, I know Paula has been divorced, but I know the story and it wasn't her fault."

I replied, "This has nothing to do with Paula White being divorced. I don't care about that."

"Then what's the problem?"

"The clearest way I can say it is that Paula White and I belong to different religions, and I don't want to be construed as endorsing her religion."

"What do you mean?"

"I mean she regularly has Donald Trump on her show—as if he has anything to do with Christianity! She's infatuated with a braggadocios playboy tycoon because he's a 'success,' a billionaire, a reality television star. But what's that got to do with Jesus?!"

That's how our conversation ended. I didn't appear on the Paula White Show and I don't regret my decision. But this is my point; in trying to communicate to my publisher the best example I could think of as to why my faith differed radically from Paula White's, I cited her fawning adulation for Donald Trump. How could you be enthralled with someone like Donald Trump *and* be a follower of Jesus? And this was all long before Donald Trump became a serious political figure.

For me, Donald Trump was the reality TV embodiment of three of the deadly sins—lust, greed, and pride. I had no reason to think the Donald Trump who openly reveled in lust, greed, and pride in his regular appearances on the Howard Stern Show would disagree with me. I have sermon notes from the 1990s where I cite Donald Trump as an example of a popular public figure who would be a poor role model for

Christians in business. That's why when I saw a young man I had led to
Jesus reading Donald Trump's *Think Big*, I took him aside and urged
him to find some better role models for his business aspirations. Why
would I do that? Because I take seriously my pastoral calling. In *Think
Big*, Donald Trump's win-at-all-cost tough guy persona is on full display
as he writes,

> The only way to get rich is to be realistic and brutally
> honest. ... It is tough, and people get hurt. So you have to
> be as tough as nails and willing to kick ass if you want to
> win. ... My motto is: Always get even. When somebody
> screws you, screw them back in spades.[1]

Nice motto. Kicking ass and getting even are acceptable if you're an
apprentice of Gordon Gekko but not if you're an apprentice of Jesus
Christ. So you can understand why I had a pastoral conversation with
my young disciple regarding his reading material. Donald Trump's
"screw them back" motto and Jesus Christ's golden rule are mutually
exclusive. But what Donald Trump advocates in his business books and
Howard Stern Show boastings is nothing particularly new; it's always
been that way in the dog-eat-dog world of ruthless competition where
everyone is reduced to winner or loser. Machiavelli set it forth
eloquently for the educated elite in *The Prince*, but Donald Trump has
an instinct for marketing the Machiavellian to the masses. It's business
as blood sport. In the end, I lost out with my young disciple—he ended
up leaving our church and calling me a "liberal false teacher." *The Art of
the Deal* trumped the Beatitudes. Again, this was all long before anyone
imagined Donald Trump becoming the champion of white
evangelicals...or the President of the United States.

The man I admire most is my father—the Honorable L. Glen
Zahnd (1931–2009). He was as unlike Donald Trump as anyone I can
imagine—humble, loyal, principled. He was a lawyer, a judge, a Sunday
School teacher, a civic leader, and most of all a wise and kind man. He
was also a very political man, a lifelong Republican. Before he became a

judge I remember him leading campaigns for a two-term governor. One of my fondest childhood memories is going with my father to the courthouse on election night to await the election returns. My dad was an ideological conservative who resonated with serious conservative thinkers like William F. Buckley and George Will. But my dad was never a fierce partisan. He admired Jimmy Carter (with whom he shared his Baptist faith) and was less than keen on Ronald Reagan. He thought Rush Limbaugh was a blowhard. My dad didn't live to see the political rise of Donald Trump, but I have no doubt what he would have thought about it. I also have no doubt what he would have done about it. (My dad led the Baptist church where he was a lifelong member out of the Southern Baptist Convention around the same time that Jimmy Carter left the SBC, and for the same reasons.)

I grew up in a political family. I know about political parties and election campaigns. But I also grew up in a Christian family where I learned about integrity, goodwill, and kindness. My father would never allow partisan politics to trump integrity, goodwill, and kindness. My dad belonged to the 19 percent.

So what happened? How did a thrice-married playboy, a braggadocios real estate tycoon, a pompous and profane reality television star win, not only the votes, but even the hearts of the vast majority of people who spent decades calling themselves the "moral majority," lecturing on "family values," and insisting that "character counts"? It's one of those "only in America" kind of stories. In *Believe Me: The Evangelical Road to Donald Trump*, evangelical scholar and Messiah College professor of history John Fea explains it like this.

> This election, while certainly unique and unprecedented in American history, is also the latest manifestation of a long-standing evangelical approach to public life. This political playbook was written in the 1970s and drew heavily from an even longer history of white evangelical fear. It is a playbook characterized by attempts to "win back" or "restore culture." It is a playbook grounded in a highly problematic interpretation of the relationship

between Christianity and the American founding. It is a playbook that too often gravitates toward nativism, xenophobia, racism, intolerance, and an unbiblical view of American exceptionalism.[2]

When authentic Christian faith is trumped by white evangelical fear, we have a problem. My ultimate concern is not for the political state of America (though I do care about this), but the spiritual state of the evangelical soul. John Fea concludes his book with these sobering words.

> Evangelicals can do better than Donald Trump. His campaign and presidency have drawn on a troubling pattern of American evangelicalism that is willing to yield to old habits grounded in fear, nostalgia, and the search for power. Too many of its leaders (and their followers) have traded their Christian witness for a mess of political pottage and a few federal judges. It should not surprise us that people are leaving evangelicalism or no longer associating themselves with that label—or, in some cases, leaving the church altogether. It's time to take a long hard look at what we have become. Believe me, we have a lot of work to do. Believe me.[3]

If evangelical support of Donald Trump is purely political—driven, for example, by a pragmatic approach to obtaining Supreme Court nominees, I may not agree with this approach, I may think it foolish and wrongheaded, even dangerous—but neither do I have a burning interest in critiquing it. I understand the rationale of the single-issue voter whose sole motive at the ballot box is to cast an anti-abortion vote. I think this approach is problematic, but I understand it. But that's not what I see happening. What I see among evangelicals—especially among some of the most prominent evangelical leaders—is an enthusiastic, uncritical, carte blanche support of Donald Trump that has more than a touch of religious aura to it. And this concerns me deeply. I'm profoundly uncomfortable when I see enthusiastic support for Donald Trump impinging upon allegiance to Jesus Christ and what he taught his followers. In April of 2016, Robert Jeffress, pastor of the twelve-thousand member Dallas First Baptist Church and Trump spiritual advisor, told the *Dallas Observer* this:

> When I'm looking for a leader who's gonna sit across the negotiating table from a nuclear Iran, or who's gonna be intent on destroying ISIS, I couldn't care less about the leader's temperament or his tone or his vocabulary. Frankly, I want the meanest, toughest son of a gun I can find. And I think that's the feeling of a lot of evangelicals. They don't want Casper Milquetoast as the leader of the free world.[4]

I too think that's the feeling of a lot of evangelicals. And that's a problem. They *don't* want a peaceable leader—a peaceable leader is denigrated as a Casper Milquetoast. Do they not want Jesus Christ as their leader as well? After all, Jesus is the Prince of Peace who teaches us to love our enemies and to turn the other cheek. Does Robert Jeffress think that the Jesus we see in the Gospels is a Casper Milquetoast? Do evangelicals really want a "tough" leader who is willing to kill their enemies on their behalf? That's Barabbas! Barabbas was a national hero and a violent revolutionary willing to kill in the name of "freedom." When you say, "I want the meanest, toughest son of a gun I can find," be careful, you might be saying, "Give us Barabbas!"

During the first year of Donald Trump's presidency CBN televangelist and founder of the Christian Coalition Pat Robertson made this outlandish statement: "The Lord's plan is being put in place for America and these people [who oppose Trump's policies] are not only revolting against Trump, they're revolting against God's plan."[5] Robertson then went on to cite a verse from Psalm 2: "The kings of the earth set themselves and the rulers take counsel together, against the LORD and his anointed."[6] The televangelist finally made the outrageous claim that Donald Trump is the Lord's anointed! Let us be clear about what Pat Robertson is doing; he is taking a Messianic passage that the Apostles, church fathers, and Christians throughout church history have claimed is fulfilled by Jesus Christ and applying it to…Donald Trump! This is idolatry. He might as well say, "We have no king but Trump." For that matter, Jim Bakker already has. Again, John Fea:

> In the United States we don't have kings, princes, or courts; but we do have our own version of religious courtiers; and many of them have what Southern Baptist theologian Richard Land has gleefully described as "unprecedented access" to the Oval Office. Disgraced televangelist Jim Bakker, now back with his own television show after being released from prison, praised prosperity preacher Paula White because she can, "walk into the White House any time she wants to" and have "full access to the King."

This leaves me speechless. So I'll let Bob Dylan say it like a poet and prophet:

> In the home of the brave
> Jefferson turnin' over in his grave
> Fools glorifying themselves, trying to manipulate Satan
> And there's a slow, slow train comin' up around the bend
>
> I don't care about economy
> I don't care about astronomy
> But it sure do bother me to see my loved ones turning into puppets
> There's a slow, slow train comin' up around the bend[7]

Again, if we're simply talking about a purely political preference, I don't have much to say about it in the context of this book. But that's not what I see. And it sure *does* bother me to see my loved ones turning into puppets! I see charismatics—people I know well and love—scrounging around in the Old Testament and making preposterous claims about Donald Trump being some kind of modern-day Cyrus. Please. Do these people not have a New Testament? Don't they know that God has raised Jesus Christ from the dead and exalted him to his right hand? Don't they know that God has given dominion over the nations to his exalted Son? Don't they know that all authority in heaven and on earth has been given to King Jesus? God may have occasionally worked his will through pagan kings in the world before Christ, but we're now living in *Anno Domini*—the year of our Lord. If you're looking for God to work his will through a pagan king (who will always coincidently belong to your political party!), I'm thinking you haven't spent much time seriously reading and digesting the New Testament epistles. God is no longer raising up pagan kings to enact his purposes, God has raised Jesus from the dead, and the fullness of God's purposes are accomplished through *him*! The Apostle Paul doesn't talk about God raising up Nero to accomplish his purposes; rather, Paul talks like this:

> God put this power to work in Christ when he raised him from the dead and seated him at his right hand in the heavenly places, far above all rule and authority and power and dominion, and above every name that is named, not only in this age but also in the age to come. And he has put all things under his feet and has made him the head over all things for the church, which is his body, the fullness of him who fills all in all.8

This is the rich Christology of Paul that should thrill our soul and inform our political theology. But if Paul's rich Christological understanding of all authority belonging to the Lord's anointed Christ isn't real to us, then we are tempted to imagine God working divine purposes through politicians who we pretend are anointed by God. This mistake can at times be relatively benign, or it can be as malignant as it was in Germany in the 1930s. There are consequences to not understanding the full ramifications of the apostolic confession that Jesus Christ is Lord.

I'm not interested in a political theology mired in a reading of the Old Testament that fails to recognize that Messiah has come. I'm a Christian and ultimately my political theology can be summed up in three words: Jesus is Lord. I'm not reading 2 Chronicles to understand how God's purposes are accomplished in the world of the 21st century AD—I'm reading Ephesians and Colossians! I'm not looking for a Cyrus—I'm looking for Christ! The resurrection of the Son of God changes everything, and if it doesn't influence our political theology, we are failing to do theology as Christians. The Hebrew Bible ends in 2 Chronicles—with Jerusalem in ruins and the people of God exiled in Babylon. (The books are arranged differently in the Christian Old Testament.) The New Testament ends in Revelation—with a flourishing New Jerusalem and Christ reigning over the nations. I'm not looking for a New Babylon where some elephant or donkey sits on the throne, I'm looking for the New Jerusalem where the Lamb sits on the throne.

The presidency of Donald Trump has been a relentless tornado of chaos. The controversies connected with Donald Trump seem to change by the hour—it's neo-Nazis having "some fine people," then it's paying off porn stars, then it's children in detention camps, then it's Putin and Russia. As I conclude the writing of this chapter, I'm on a flight from Toronto, and for all I know what I've written will be out of date by the time I land in Kansas City; I'm certain it will be out of date by the time this book is published. But I write it anyway. I write it in memory of my father. I write it so I'll be on record. I write it so my grandchildren will know that during the Trump era I wasn't duped, I wasn't silent, and I didn't go along for the ride. I want them to know that I saw what was happening, I knew it for what it was, and I spoke out.

The Joke's On Caesar

Caesar and God
Caesar or God
Caesar vs. God
Both call for my allegiance
Jesus said give each their due
But who gets what—how do I divvy it up?
Roman Christian or Christian Roman?
American Christian or Christian American?
Who gets to be the noun?
And who gets relegated to adjective duty?
Here's something I'm coming to know—
Christian is a great noun
But a lousy adjective
Now we're on to something
Here's what I learned from history
And the prophets
Caesar tries to tell me
Hey, it's all the same
Because God is Caesar's God
Believe me
(Nationalization of the divine!)
"God shed her grace on thee"
"One nation under God"
"In God we trust"
So the question is solved
Give your all to Caesar
Ask not what Caesar can do for you…
And don't worry your pretty little head about competing
　　　allegiance
Because Caesar is the authorized middle man
Between God and the common man

Civil Religion and Social Contract
Like Rousseau said
And it doesn't even matter if there's really no deity in the
    temple at all
But the prophets cry foul!
The earth is mine
Your thoughts are not my thoughts
Your ways are not my ways
Your government is not my government
Thus saith the Lord
Render unto Caesar
What?
Taxes
But not heart and soul and mind and strength
Let Caesar police the streets and fix the pot holes
But don't ask for much more
Let Caesar be a custodian of civility
Anything more tends to idolatry
Render unto God
Total allegiance
And what's left for Caesar?
Not much
And that's how it should be
A denarii for Caesar
To fix the pot hole and pay the constable
To make life a little more livable
But heart and soul
Are pledged to Christ and the government of God
Kyrios Christos
Ianitor Caesar
But does Caesar resent demotion to custodian?
You betcha
Caesar is proud
And always has the nature of a beast
So don't feed him very much

Because when he gets big, bad things happen
Some were sawn asunder
While the patriotic cheered
And why did they cheer?
Because Caesar is a seasoned politician
Who knows how to campaign
Which means to promise
Which means to lie
A chicken in every pot
Charity begins at home
It's the economy, stupid
Mission accomplished
Our rightful place in the world
The last best hope of earth
Manifest destiny
We're #1!
Make America Great Again
Just do what we say and nobody gets hurt
If only Jesus would campaign like that
Take up your cross and follow me
Turn the other cheek
The way is hard
Who's gonna vote for that?
What do you mean it's not a democratic process?
Promoted to the Oval Office of the Universe?
By whom?
By God!
For life!
Caesar's not going to like that
Nor the puppet master pulling Caesar's strings
That reminds me
Did you ever notice they all say the same thing?
Our great nation
Our great cause
Our great destiny

Nebuchadnezzar did it best
The freakin' megalomaniac
Drove himself insane
A sense of humor is the surest sign of sanity
But Caesar never sees what's so funny
Because the joke's on him
Let's hear a laugh for the man of the world
Who thinks he can make things work
Tried to build a New Jerusalem
And ended up with New York
Bruce Cockburn said that
Ha!
Count on a Canadian to laugh at the empire
Laughter's good for the soul
And good for your sanity
So keep on laughing
And loving
And longing
And looking
For the city whose builder and maker is God
For the New Jerusalem
And the Lamb who is her light

CHAPTER 10

POSTCARDS FROM BABYLON

By the rivers of Babylon—
there we sat down and wept
when we remembered Zion.
—Psalm 137:1

We should all have a monastery. We should all have a sacred space we can frequent now and then to bathe our world-weary souls in an atmosphere of prayer and peace. Of course there is the solace found in wilderness places. Unspoiled deserts, mountains, forests, lakes, and, if you can find them, un-crowded beaches can be cathedrals in their own way. In the spirit of John Muir I know this is true. I find my solace of wild places in the Rocky Mountains; it's always good for my soul to spend time in the cathedral of nature far from the madding crowd. But I've also found it's good to have some connection with a real, living monastery. Monasteries are gentle reminders that in a cutthroat competitive world there are contemplative alternatives to the rat race. So I like spending a few days in the peaceful quiet of a sacred place dedicated to the ancient traditions and practices of Christian prayer and worship. "My" monastery is Conception Abbey—a Benedictine monastery in rural Northwest Missouri founded by Swiss monks in 1872 which today is home to sixty-five brothers. I like to go there for a few days and slide into the Benedictine rhythm of prayer—Vigils, Lauds, Eucharist, Vespers, Compline. Occasionally I'm the only guest among the monks for a particular prayer service—or as I like to think of it, a sixty-sixth temporary monk. The guest master charged with looking after me during my stays often displays a good-humored exasperation with my inability to pick the correct prayer book for the appointed service, shaking his head in feigned vexation as he hands me the right one. I like that monk.

In 2017, I was spending three days at the monastery, not writing, not working, not even reading anything (other than Scripture and some brief meditations by Henri Nouwen). I was there to pray—both participating in the monastic rhythm of communal prayer and spending long periods of time in personal prayer. During the afternoons I would pray while making two or three circuits around the two-mile walking trail on the monastery grounds. On my final afternoon I was beginning the last lap of my long walk when I became increasingly troubled about the awful truth that so much of the American church has been captured by an ugly religious nationalism. As I walked I sensed that this burden was not one I had carried into the monastery, rather it was a burden that came to me while in the monastery. In other words, this was a burden I was *supposed* to feel. I wasn't on a three-day spiritual retreat to jettison this burden; I was there to receive this burden. As I continued the final two miles of the circuit there was a moment while walking beside a lake—I remember the precise spot—when I asked myself, "What should I do?" The response came quickly and from somewhere deep inside: "It's time to write some postcards from Babylon." That's what this book is.

If American Christians imagine America as a kind of Biblical Israel, we will inevitably make the mistake of thinking that the apparatuses of American government—including the war machine—are commissioned by God for divine purposes. Thus to "Make America Great Again" is imagined to be supported by divine warrant and connected to the salvation of the world. But America is not a kind of Biblical Israel— America is a kind of biblical Babylon. America is the latest in a long line of Babylons. In many ways America is the natural successor to the Babylon that was the British Empire. I don't mean this as an ugly pejorative but as a sober, dispassionate analysis. America *may* be a kinder, gentler Babylon, but it's a Babylon nonetheless. Realizing this makes an enormous difference.

A number of years ago I was in Paris preaching in one of the largest evangelical churches in France and teaching in their Bible college. Over lunch the pastor of the church asked what I would be teaching on in the Bible college; I told him I wanted to talk for three days on the kingdom of God. He said, "Oh, don't do that!" When I asked why, he replied, "Because Americans all think the United States is the kingdom of God." I assured the pastor I would not make that mistake, but I understood his entirely legitimate reaction. Many American pastors, preachers, and teachers *have* conflated the United States and the kingdom of God, and they've done it in ways that, not coincidently, always support the national interests of the United States. These American Christian leaders don't do this in a calculating way; it's just what happens if you can't perceive the radical difference between what Jesus meant by the kingdom of God and what Thomas Jefferson dreamt of in 1776. A conflation of God and country can bump along benignly enough for a time, but when the country takes a dark turn toward nationalism and nativism, things can get ugly in a hurry. And that's what has happened.

The saving grace will be found in a Spirit-received revelation that America is a kind of Babylon, not a kind of Israel. This perspective doesn't mean we have to have a disdainful antagonism toward America any more than it meant Daniel had to have a disdainful antagonism toward Babylon. But it does mean we must always be prepared to spend a night in the lion's den if our allegiance to national interest comes into conflict with our allegiance to God's kingdom—and we should operate from the assumption that from time to time these allegiances *will* come into conflict.

So it's from Babylon that I write my postcards—postcards addressed to the bride of Christ I love so dearly. I write with an urgency but not in despair; I write with an edge but not in anger; I write with passion but not with cynicism. I only want to say what the prophets and apostles have always said, "Babylon is fallen," just as the apostles have always said that Christ is risen. It's not a Babylon that God has raised—not even one of the stars and stripes variety. It is Christ alone whom God has raised. Babylon is fallen and always falling, but Christ is eternally risen.

About ten years ago N.T. Wright gave a series of lectures on the book of Acts at a pastor's conference in San Diego. He concluded his lectures with these words:

> And it is only now, now that we have the whole sweep of the book of Acts before us that we can see where we are today, why we have arrived at this point, and perhaps even where we must go. We know that we've got to get to Caesar with the gospel, we know today far better than many generations that we have to announce to the principalities and powers that their time is up, that Jesus is Lord and they are not. That the unchecked power of mammon is an idol that has to be named and shamed. That the seductive enticements of Aphrodite are a ghastly lie which must be refuted and resisted. That the horrid trumpets of the war god Mars appeal to all that is worst in us and will make the world a worse place. We know all this. We know we must resist paganism in all these forms in the name of Jesus the crucified and risen Lord. And we are to bring this message to bear, locally and globally. We are not a complacent church. We are struggling to be a faithful church.[1]

I believe in struggling to be a faithful church. It's what I've spent my entire adult life doing. The struggle to be a faithful church is real—especially when the church is planted in a modern-day Babylon. But the possibility to be a faithful church is real too, and I believe in the possibility of a faithful church with all my heart. My life-defining faith in Jesus Christ not only *includes* faith in the church but *requires* faith in the church. For Jesus Christ himself said that he is the one building his church and that the gates of hell and death will not prevail against it. I believe this as surely as I believe Christ is risen from the dead. So, yes, I believe in a church triumphant—not triumphant in the manner of crusaders and conquerors but triumphant in the manner of the crucified Christ. Jesus doesn't call his disciples to stand on the sidelines and merely watch what he does with his cross. Jesus calls his disciples to take up their own cross and follow him in faithful imitation. Nothing less is authentic discipleship.

The call to take up your cross and follow Christ in the way of co-suffering love will always be a tough sell to those living in a superpower enthralled with conventional greatness, but there will always be those who hear and dare to heed that call. I am privileged to know some of these countercultural Christians. Many of them are young and seem to have an immunity to the virulent virus of religious nationalism. Some of them are seminarians deeply passionate about reading the Bible as a counter-imperial text. Some of them are young energetic church planters willing to rethink what a faithful congregation looks like in an increasingly post-Christian society. Some of them are still in their teens but, like me so long ago, they have had an encounter with Christ so captivating that it will determine how they live the rest of their lives. These seminarians, church planters, and teenage disciples whom I have met give me hope. Babylon may pose a challenge, but Babylon never has the final say, because Babylon is fallen. It is Christ who is the eternal Word of the Father, and it is Christ who is risen. So shine on, Bride of Christ—even in Babylon shine on! Amidst the lies and idols of Babylon, let us hold forth the Word of Life as we hold to the mystery of our faith—a faith that always has the power to again and again turn the world upside down.

Christ has died.
Christ is risen.
Christ will come again.

POSTCARDS FROM BABYLON PLAYLIST

This forty-song playlist is the soundtrack for *Postcards From Babylon*. The songs appear in a chronological order connected with the book. With some songs the reader can easily see the connection to *Postcards From Babylon*, with other songs perhaps only I understand the connection. In any case, the music is good. I have created a public Spotify playlist for those interested in listening to the music. Enjoy.

1. Tangled Up In Blue – Bob Dylan
2. Black Dog – Led Zeppelin
3. Waves – Rez Band
4. The Great American Novel – Larry Norman
5. Ohio – Crosby, Stills, Nash & Young
6. I'm Gonna Be (500 Miles) – The Proclaimers
7. It's Alright Ma (I'm Only Bleeding) – Bob Dylan
8. Idiot Wind – Bob Dylan
9. Bombs Below – Living Things
10. Sea of Heartbreak – Johnny Cash
11. Tumbling Dice – The Rolling Stones
12. Sweet Virginia – The Rolling Stones
13. Palestine Texas – T Bone Burnett
14. Seven Times Hotter Than Fire – T Bone Burnett
15. Laughter – Bruce Cockburn
16. It's Going Down Slow – Bruce Cockburn
17. I Love Portugal – Sun Kil Moon

18. Cortez the Killer – Neil Young
19. Satan Your Kingdom Must Come Down – Robert Plant
20. Jokerman – Bob Dylan
21. Angelina – Bob Dylan
22. Walk It Back – The National
23. The System Only Dreams In Total Darkness – The National
24. Easter Song – Keith Green
25. The Song of Jesus – Jason Upton
26. Feel It All Around – Washed Out
27. Seasons (Waiting On You) – Future Islands
28. Demons – The National
29. All Along The Watchtower – Jimi Hendrix
30. Every Time I Feel the Shift – T Bone Burnett
31. With God On Our Side – Bob Dylan
32. In My Time of Dying – Led Zeppelin
33. Slow Train – Bob Dylan
34. Nettie Moore – Bob Dylan
35. Saint Of Me – The Rolling Stones
36. Love Is All We Have Left – U2
37. American Soul – U2
38. You Want It Darker – Leonard Cohen
39. Goodbye Babylon – The Black Keys
40. 13 (There Is A Light) – U2

Endnotes

Chapter 1: Conversion, Catacombs, and a Counterculture

[1] Luke 14:33

[2] Revelation 18:2–5

[3] Acts 24:14 (NLT)

[4] Revelation 17:5

[5] Revelation 11:15

[6] See Luke 19:41–44

[7] Romans 13:4

[8] Romans 13:1

[9] See John 18:36

[10] Romans 12:21

[11] Revelation 12:11

Chapter 2: A Camino of Crucifixes

[1] Bob Dylan, "It's Alright, Ma (I'm Only Bleeding), *Bringing It All Back Home*

[2] Galatians 3:1 (ESV)

[3] 1 Corinthians 2:2

[4] Philippians 2:6–11

[5] See 1 Corinthians 1:22–25

[6] See Colossians 2:15

[7] N.T. Wright, *The Day the Revolution Began* (New York: HarperCollins, 2016), 407.

[8] 2 Corinthians 12:7

[9] Isaiah 53:4 (CSB)

[10] 1 Peter 2:24

[11] Depending on how you translate *parepidemos* in 1 Peter 1:1.

[12] 1 Peter 5:13 (NLT)

[13] See Isaiah 21:9, Jeremiah 51:44–49, Revelation 14:8, Revelation 18:2

[14] 1 Peter 2:22–24 (NLT)

[15] 1 Peter 2:21

[16] René Girard, *Battling to the End: Conversations with Benoît Chantre* (East Lansing, MI: Michigan State University Press, 2019), 18.

[17] See Revelation 6.

[18] 1 Peter 2:23

[19] 1 Peter 2:24

[20] Fyodor Dostoevsky, *Crime and Punishment, translated by Constance Garnett* (Norwalk, CT: Easton Press, 1966), 365.

Chapter 3: Tangled Up in Red, White, and Blue

[1] William T. Cavanaugh, *Migrations of the Holy: God, State, and the Political Meaning of the Church* (Grand Rapids, MI: Eerdmans 2011), 168.

[2] Alan Kreider, *The Patient Ferment of the Early Church: The Improbable Rise of Christianity in the Roman Empire* (Grand Rapids, MI: Baker Academic, 2016), 29.

[3] Kreider, 120

[4] John 18:36

[5] Ephesians 6:12

[6] Kreider, 118

[7] Matthew 6:24

[8] John 19:15 (ESV)

[9] Luke 14:26

[10] Matthew 26:42

[11] David Bentley Hart, "No Enduring City," *A Splendid Wickedness and Other Essays* (Grand Rapids, MI: Eerdmans, 2016), 226.

Chapter 4: Exile on Main Street

[1] Kreider, 98

[2] Kreider, 99

[3] Rowan Williams, "The Two Ways" in *Plough Quarterly No.14 Autumn 2017* https://www.plough.com/en/topics/faith/discipleship/the-two-ways-williams

⁴ Jeremiah 29:1, 4–7

⁵ Deuteronomy 6:4–5 (ESV)

⁶ Daniel 1:15 (NLT)

⁷ Matthew 12:34

⁸ Matthew 6:21

⁹ Psalm 20:7 (ESV)

¹⁰ John 18:11 (NIV)

¹¹ Daniel 2:1 (NLT)

¹² See Daniel 2:31–45

¹³ Daniel 2:44

¹⁴ Isaiah 2:2

¹⁵ Matthew 19:30

¹⁶ Daniel 3:1

¹⁷ Daniel 3:6 (NLT)

¹⁸ Daniel 3:8–12

¹⁹ Daniel 3:16–18

²⁰ Daniel 3:19 (NLT)

²¹ Daniel 3:25 (KJV)

²² Revelation 18:4

Chapter 5: In the Time of Tyrant Kings

¹ Matthew 2:1

² http://ngm.nationalgeographic.com/2008/12/herod/mueller-text/3

³ Matthew 2:3

⁴ Rosa Brooks, *How Everything Became War and the Military Became Everything: Tales from the Pentagon* (New York, NY: Simon & Schuster, 2016), 105.

⁵ Stanley Hauerwas, *Brazos Theological Commentary on the Bible: Matthew* (Grand Rapids, MI: Brazos Press, 2006), 38.

⁶ Matthew 2:17–18

⁷ See Jeremiah 31:15

⁸ Hauerwas, 37

⁹ John 1:5

[10] Revelation 12:10–11

[11] Acts 11:26

[12] Kreider, 8

[13] 1 John 4:18

[14] Hauerwas, 38

[15] See Matthew 4:23, 9:25, 24:14

[16] Mark 1:14–15, (MSG)

[17] Matthew 3:2

[18] Mark 1:15

[19] Matthew 11:12 (NLT, marginal rendering)

[20] Mark 10:32

[21] Mark 10:33–34

[22] Hosea 6:2

[23] Luke 13:32

Chapter 6: There's Always Some Dude on a Horse

[1] Proverbs 21:31

[2] Exodus 15:1

[3] Joshua 11:6

[4] Deuteronomy 17:16

[5] 2 Chronicles 9:25

[6] Psalm 20:7

[7] Isaiah 2:4

[8] Isaiah 2:5–8 (NLT, emphasis added)

[9] Zechariah 9:9–10

[10] Walter Brueggemann, *The Prophetic Imagination* (Minneapolis, MN: Fortress Press, 2001), 40.

[11] Zechariah 9:12

[12] Luke 19:37–38

[13] Matthew 21:10

[14] Luke 19:39–40

[15] Luke 19:41–44

[16] Translated by Robert Fagles, *The Iliad / Homer* (New York: Viking, 1990), 77.

[17] Fagles, 614

[18] Fagles, 589

[19] Lisa Peterson, Dennis O'Hare, *An Iliad* (The Overlook Press: New York, 2014), pp. 79–87

[20] Freya Stark, *Rome on the Euphrates: The Story of a Frontier* (Tauris Park Paperbacks: London, 2012), 29

[21] "Anchors Aweigh," lyrics by George D. Lottman, 1926

[22] Matthew 7:21

[23] Brian Zahnd, *Sinners in the Hands of a Loving God,* Colorado Springs, CO: WaterBrook, 2017.

[24] Revelation 22:20–21

Chapter 7: Satan, Your Kingdom Must Come Down

[1] Isaiah 14:12 (KJV)

[2] David Bentley Hart, *The New Testament: A Translation* (New Haven, CT: Yale University Press, 2001), 474.

[3] Psalm 2:8

[4] 1 Timothy 6:15, Revelation 17:14, Revelation 19:16

[5] See Daniel 2:37

[6] Revelation 12:1–5

[7] Psalm 2:2

[8] Isaiah 14:13–14

[9] Daniel 4:30

[10] Daniel 4:27 (NLT) (emphasis added)

[11] Daniel 4:13 (KJV)

[12] "Faith, Certainty, and the Presidency of George W. Bush," New York Times *Magazine,* October 17, 2004

https://www.nytimes.com/2004/10/17/magazine/faith-certainty-and-the-presidency-of-george-w-bush.html

[13] Isaiah 14:7–8 (NLT)

[14] Isaiah 14:9–12a (NLT)

[15] Isaiah 14:16–17

[16] Isaiah 14:23 (NIV)

[17] Isaiah 21:9 and Revelation 14:8

[18] Mark 1:23–24 (NLT)

[19] See John 12:31, John 16:11, 1 Corinthians 15:24, 2 Corinthians 4:4, Revelation 11:15

[20] Genesis 4:7 (NIV)

[21] 1 John 3:8 (NASB)

[22] Matthew 12:28

[23] Hauerwas, 51

[24] 1 Peter 5:8 (ESV)

[25] Hebrews 11:10

[26] "continuall feare, and danger of violent death; And the life of man, solitary, poore, nasty, brutish, and short" Thomas Hobbes, *Leviathan* (London: Penguin Books, 1651, 1985), 186.

[27] *The Thin Red Line*, screenplay by Terrence Malick, 20th Century Fox, 1998

[28] G.K. Chesterton, *The Everlasting Man* (San Francisco: Ignatius Press, 1925, 1993), 213.

[29] "US attorney general quotes Bible to defend separating families" BBC News, June 15, 2018 https://www.bbc.com/news/world-us-canada-44499048

[30] Matthew 27:65–66

[31] Matthew 28:1–4 (ESV)

[32] 2 Corinthians 5:7

[33] Revelation 21:5 (ESV)

Chapter 8: Feel the Falseness

[1] Matthew 7:26–27

[2] John 8:44–46

[3] See John 8:31–36

[4] John 8:59

[5] John 18:37 (ESV)

[6] John 18:38

[7] John 19:10

[8] John 19:15

[9] John 18:36

[10] Jude 1:11

[11] Proverbs 23:23

[12] "Christians More Supportive of Torture Than Non-Religious Americans" by Sarah Posner, Religious Dispatches, December 16, 2014 http://religiondispatches.org/christians-more-supportive-of-torture-than-non-religious-americans/

[13] *Gott Mit Uns* (God With Us) was inscribed on Nazi belt buckles.

[14] Matthew 4:8 (ESV)

[15] Joshua 5:13–14 (NIV)

[16] Joshua 24:15

[17] Luke 9:60

[18] Ecclesiastes 3:3, 8

Chapter 9: Trumped

[1] Donald J. Trump, *Think Big: Make It Happen in Business and Life* (New York: HarperBusiness, 2008), 2, 169.

[2] John Fea, *Believe Me: The Evangelical Road to Donald Trump* (Grand Rapids, MI: Eerdmans, 2018), 6–7.

[3] Fea, 190–191

[4] Fea, 39

[5] "Pat Robertson says people against Trump are 'revolting against God's plan'",

HillReporter.com, February 16, 2017 https://hillreporter.com/pat-robertson-says-people-trump-revolting-gods-plan-300

[6] Psalm 2:2

[7] "Slow Train" by Bob Dylan, Special Rider Music, 1979

[8] Ephesians 1:20–23

Chapter 10: Postcards from Babylon

[1] This quote is from the notes of Joe Beach who attended the conference, and to the best of my knowledge, do not appear in print anywhere else.

Made in the USA
Middletown, DE
31 January 2019